D0350334

LEARNING JOURNEYS

*Top Management Experts Share
Hard-Earned Lessons on Becoming
Great Mentors and Leaders*

Editors

MARSHALL GOLDSMITH

BEVERLY KAYE

KEN SHELTON

DAVIES-BLACK PUBLISHING PALO ALTO, CALIFORNIA

Published by Davies-Black Publishing, an imprint of Consulting Psychologists Press, Inc., 3803 East Bayshore Road, Palo Alto, CA 94303; 800-624-1765.

Special discounts on bulk quantities of Davies-Black books are available to corporations, professional associations, and other organizations. For details, contact the Director of Book Sales at Davies-Black Publishing, an imprint of Consulting Psychologists Press, Inc., 3803 East Bayshore Road, Palo Alto, CA 94303; 650-691-9123; fax 650-623-9271.

Copyright © 2000 by Marshall Goldsmith, Beverly Kaye, and Ken Shelton. All rights reserved. No part of this book may be reproduced, stored in a retrieval system, or transmitted in any form or by any means, electronic, mechanical, photocopying, recording, or otherwise, without written permission of the publisher, except in the case of brief quotations embodied in critical articles or reviews.

Cover image: Olivier Garros/Photonica

Davies-Black and colophon are registered trademarks of Consulting Psychologists Press, Inc.

Visit the Davies-Black Publishing web site at www.daviesblack.com.

04 03 02 01 00   10 9 8 7 6 5 4 3 2 1

Printed in the United States of America

Library of Congress Cataloging-in-Publication Data

Learning journeys : top management experts share hard-earned lessons on becoming great mentors and leaders / editors, Marshall Goldsmith, Beverly Kaye, Ken Shelton.—1st ed.
    p. cm.
    This book is one product of a Learning Network, a weekend conference, held in Del Mar, California, in January.
    ISBN 0-89106-147-9
    1. Executives—Training of—Congresses. 2. Leadership—Study and teaching—Congresses. 3. Mentoring in business—Congresses. 4. Storytelling—Congresses. I. Goldsmith, Marshall. II. Kaye, Beverly. III. Shelton, Ken
    HD30.4 .L396 2000
    658.4'07124—dc21
                                                                00-031438

FIRST EDITION
First printing 2000

Contents

DEVELOPING SELF-KNOWLEDGE

UNLEARNING WHAT YOU THOUGHT WAS SO

PAIN IS A GREAT TEACHER

Preface

For several years now, for one weekend every January, a senior group of thought leaders in the field of management and organization development have come together as a Learning Network. The weekend, held in beautiful Del Mar, California, is devoted to learning how our work interconnects, thinking about the future, and designing projects that enable us to "give back" to the world. Numerous ideas have been generated at these retreats, and while many have never made it off the brainstorming table, several have lasted and made a positive difference.

This book is a product of one of those weekends. In a brainstorming session we decided to focus on how we learned. This was quite different from our "normal" work—helping others learn! We also came up with the idea of editing this book. Not only could we learn from each other, but we could learn from a great sample of many of the thought leaders in our field. The idea of learning how great teachers learn fascinated us!

During the weekend we decided to donate royalties from the book to the Peter Drucker Foundation for Nonprofit Management. The Foundation does great work in providing leadership resources and development opportunities. It also provides a forum for thought leaders in our field to share their latest ideas.

One of the founding members of the Learning Network was Dick Beckhard. Dick was a true leader in our field and, more important, a wonderful human being. He greatly supported us in this and many of our other efforts. We felt it appropriate to dedicate this book to Dick.

The editors/authors, who spearheaded this effort, gathered others to join us and share in this project. What started as a collectible book of stories about the people in that room (a bit easier to get one's arms around) became a much larger collection of stories of leaders and thinkers who made significant contributions to the field of management development. Lists were drawn; networks were shared; and calls were made. The work began, and what seemed like an easy job in the beginning became . . . a journey in and of itself!

When we asked 100 of the most prominent figures in the field of management and organization development to describe a personal learning experience—a "marker" that shaped their life's work and influenced their teachings—we got some amazing stories.

And these leaders became real.

In these stories they come to life as coaches and mentors, and we identify with both their genius and their humanness. They teach the value of self-knowledge and reflection. They motivate us to discover and describe our own "learning journeys," to find our own voices, to uncover our own answers, and to share our stories with others.

Everyone's life is filled with experiences—traumatic, rewarding, frustrating, and humiliating. All can be sources of valuable learning. Some people are more adept at reflecting on the meaning of these experiences than others, but we all understand the power of storytelling. We enjoy reading about people: their stories tap our emotions and intellects, helping us remember and learn.

Those management thinkers see learning as a process; they retell their personal stories to offer fresh insights, uncover new challenges, and lead others to contribute more of their full potential.

This book suggests that all of us can learn to examine our lives, reflect on our successes and failures, and tune in to the music of our own stories. We can look to experiences in our lives for wisdom and guidance.

As we read the stories of this collection, we find many things we can directly relate to, or at least empathize with, from our own experiences and thoughts. More than abstract concepts, these stories make for enjoyable, memorable reading that leads to greater insight.

We hope these learning journeys, along with the personal reflection questions asked by each storyteller in this book, will help unearth greater meaning for people in families, groups, businesses, governments, and communities. We hope that this book will help you learn from the stories that unfold in your own life!

A PERSONAL NOTE

Beverly Kaye has truly been the "heart and soul" of this *Learning Journeys* project. She originated the idea, developed the concept, and helped us all "hang in there" until the project was successfully completed. Without her ongoing drive, support, and inspiration, this book would have never happened.

One of my great learning journeys has been the opportunity to work with Bev on this project. She has an amazing spirit that is contagious. She never lets day-to-day hassles get her down or remove her joy in her profession and her life. She has the gift of making every day seem like a wonderful learning journey!

Speaking for everyone who has contributed to making this book a reality, I would like to say "Thank you!" to Beverly Kaye.

Marshall Goldsmith
July 2000

Acknowledgments

One could never begin the acknowledgments in a book of stories without a special thank-you to the storytellers. Each story you read in this book either was collected by personal interview or was written by the storyteller. Each contributor gave time and trust, and each probed deeply to help us find the nugget of information that might be the most telling and the most useful to readers. And for every story that appears on these pages, there were many more that ended, sadly, on the cutting room floor. Alas, the book could accommodate only so many stories. To the contributors whose stories we treasure but were unable to include in this edition: we thank you as well.

The second thank-you goes to another large group—the Del Mar Learning Network. The noted authors and management thinkers in this group were the first to support and participate in our effort and to applaud it along the way. They continue to gather for their yearly meetings and contribute to the world of business in a multitude of ways.

The next group is smaller. We've called them the "weavers." They asked for the stories, listened to the stories, and tried their best to retell the stories so that each contribution remained true to its originator. They wove the stories into a book, and it was not an easy job. We were fortunate to have the hands, heads, and hearts of Alaine Weiss, Cindy Miller, and Leanne Rubinstein to support us in this endeavor.

If the truth be told, the burden fell on certain backs more than others. Jodi Knox came to the project as she was completing her doctorate at the California School of Professional Psychology; she undertook a majority of the interviews and helped to coordinate the project from its inception. She was inspirational in her belief in the power of story and of the importance of properly using stories in the business setting. Milo Sindell picked up where Jodi left off when she moved to New York City. Milo was completing his master's degree at Pepperdine, and he put in many, many hours, not only weaving, but also taking care of the many inevitable details. Milo is a believer in the importance of legacy, and he saw the project as a way to help the storytellers leave a part of themselves to others. Dale Ironson stayed with the project as well. Dale conducted interviews, participated in the conceptual work, and wrote a chapter with Jodi on the power of this process. All who participated in the interviewing agreed on one thing: the process was an awesome, instructive, and life-changing event.

Marshall Goldsmith led the charge. With his positive (life is good!) attitude, he kept us going when we thought the work had become overwhelming. Marshall never doubted the importance of this book, never doubted that we would complete it, and never doubted that it would sell! His enthusiasm, his networking abilities, and his courage kept it on track. Ken Shelton contributed his editorial savvy and some of the superb storytellers from his Executive Excellence and Personal Excellence network.

And so the project became a process. I came with the idea, but with no conception of its size and scope. I served as a catalyst to move the idea forward and worked the trenches to keep the larger team on course. I had no conception of all that I would learn about myself, about collaboration, and about the amazing powers of my colleagues and teachers whose stories appear on these pages. The growth of this book took about three years (and I thought it would take six months!). It taught all who were associated with it. We hope it teaches you.

Beverly Kaye

Introduction
Using Stories of Learning and Leadership

This is a book for managers, leaders, coaches, and consultants. The stories told here by top management thought leaders contain powerful lessons from their own learning journeys. Many of the lessons were learned outside the classroom and outside of work, for leadership lessons are wherever we find them, and that is, as often as not, outside the organizations we serve. As the stories demonstrate, truly effective people learn from all of life and learn all their lives long. We hope that looking at managerial challenges—how to manage ourselves first and foremost and then how to lead others—in settings outside of work will make the lessons go down just a little easier by sliding them around the routines and defenses that we build up to handle the stresses of organizational life. These are stories that we can connect with on a human level.

During the past decade, business leaders, trainers, and consultants have discovered the power of storytelling as a serious and indispensable management and leadership tool. The literature on this topic is quickly expanding. Important books such as Howard Gardner's *Leading Minds* and *The Leadership Engine* by Noel Tichy have taken storytelling from the classroom and put it into the boardrooms of major corporations. Numerous articles in business publications such as *Fortune, FastCompany,* the *Wall Street Journal,* and the *Harvard Business Review* explore the many applications of storytelling to issues such as strategic planning, leader development, corporate communications, sales, learning, and knowledge management.

Leading authorities in many professions and academic arenas are realizing that it is important to adopt a continuous learning paradigm rather than rest on one's laurels. Stories inspired by personal experiences help bring the learning process to life. This is especially so when the stories are told, as they are here, by our best management leaders, trainers, and consultants.

USING STORIES TO LEAD AND TO TEACH

In our work as trainers, we have learned that experience is the best teacher. Training is designed to cause an "aha!" moment. But instead of just one such moment, imagine many of them, prompted by each participant's story. We can learn more from the collective knowledge of a group of people than by tapping into the experience of one individual. All of us have experiences that are interesting and valuable to those around us. The key is to find ways to unlock and harness this learning potential.

The power of story is alive in the lessons each of us share and use in our day-to-day lives. Many of the stories in this book will resonate on a personal level for particular individuals, and some stories can serve as general lessons for us all.

Following are suggestions for furthering self-exploration and insight. While each story in this book poses its own questions, here we want to bring out some of the overarching themes and inquiries suggested by the chapters. Each section below corresponds to a section of the book and offers a list of questions that can be applied in a group setting for team building or as possible icebreakers. And of course, these questions can be a continuation of your own exploration or perhaps a dialogue starter for your own group of friends. Use them for inspiration, as a resource, or as a starting point. The exercises are intended as springboards for your own ideas and creativity. We hope they will help you in your own learning journey and encourage you to use stories to share knowledge, to develop mutual understanding, and to build deeper appreciation for differences.

LESSONS ON LEADERSHIP

Learning to live our own lives effectively often provides the most powerful lessons on leadership. After all, if we cannot be leaders for ourselves, how can we be leaders for others? And for others to trust us as leaders, they must know us; they must see our true selves. That means that we must know and be willing to reveal our true selves. Authenticity requires us to be true to ourselves as well as to others—true in our conversations, our behaviors, and our intentions. Significant events or individuals in our lives can enable us to find our true voice and feelings, and getting to our personal truths can be a valuable journey toward leadership. Nancy Dixon, in her book *Perspectives on Dialogue,* suggests how difficult this is in organizational life: "I believe that people long for a more authentic kind of interaction with their co-workers but they are not sure that it is possible, or even if their longing is legitimate. Work is not generally thought of as a place where you are supposed to get your own needs met. Thus, people come to accept what they believe to be inevitable: that they must leave a part of themselves at home when they come to work."

Consider your own journey to authenticity and leadership:

In your life's story, are you your own author? What kind of life are you writing?

What has been your experience regarding the discovery of your authentic self?

Were there key players or events that were significant?

What are some situations in which it has been difficult to be authentic as a leader?

What is the downside to not being true to yourself and to others?

How do you nurture authenticity in your relationships?

CROSSROADS AND CHOICES

Robert Frost said it best. That fork in the road presents itself almost every day, and we must make a choice. Our natural tendency may be to take a well-worn path, but we can experiment and explore the new. All paths can lead to learning and personal growth, and in fact, sometimes it is the more mundane choices that have the most impact. Our decisions involve what kind of mood to be in, how to treat people, how to treat ourselves, and what to do with our lives. Big choices are often so difficult that they become painful, but of course we all know that not to decide is a decision in itself.

Consider the following questions about your life crossroads:

What have been major decision points in your life? What prompted one of these decisions?

What have been your experiences with making pivotal choices that worked out well? Describe one that didn't turn out well.

How can you help others learn to make better choices and to accept the choices they make?

Who has helped you make the best decisions, and how have these people been influences?

How do you make choices about your life? Do you involve others? Do you labor silently? What have you learned about your choices that will be helpful to tell others?

LEADING, LEARNING, AND TEACHING

It is interesting (and one of the underlying premises of this collection of stories) that the best teachers are those who never stop learning. The difficult issue for most is whether and how to move continually back and forth between teaching and learning. And how does one gain the insight to know when both opportunities present themselves? Parker Palmer in *The Courage to Teach* says,

"In every class I teach, my ability to connect with my students, and to connect them with the subject, depends less on the methods I use than on the degree to which I know and trust my selfhood—and am willing to make it available and vulnerable in the service of learning."

Consider the following questions to check your ability to be an "expert":

Reflecting on times you have taught, consider what you learned. What knowledge was reinforced? What new knowledge or abilities did you discover?

What are the different environments that you utilize to teach others? What opportunities exist in your life now to take advantage of learning by teaching others?

What are your stories about significant learning experiences you have had while engaged in teaching others?

SEEING YOURSELF AS OTHERS DO

When we are able to step back, watch what is occurring around us, and see ourselves from the perspectives of others, we are using our "third eye." Stepping back enables us to see things in a broader view. Often we are so caught up with the politics and emotions of what is happening in our lives that we are unable to relax and gain this larger view, but when we slow down and see things from another perspective, great clarity and learning can occur.

Consider the following questions related to this "third eye" learning experience:

When do you pause to reflect on your life and the factors that contribute to current events and situations?

Describe a scenario in which your perspective changed when you stepped back.

Can you teach others to step back in order to experience an objective perspective? How?

In the heat of the moment it can be difficult to step outside the situation and see things from a broad perspective. How do you remind yourself to breathe and take a look around before proceeding?

DEVELOPING SELF-KNOWLEDGE

Surpassing the limits that confine us entails taking risks, and sometimes it takes what others see in us to provide us with the confidence we need to take those risks. Has anyone ever told you that you were great at something you were insecure about? Their words probably gave you the confidence you needed to try a little harder, to become a little more than you otherwise would have. Because discovering our potential means exploring the unknown, it means taking chances, and sometimes it means making mistakes, but if we don't try, if we don't risk failure, we will not reach our potential.

Consider the following questions as you think about the risks you've taken:

When do you pause to reflect on your life and the factors that currently contribute to it? As you reflect, what do you find that is valuable? What can you do in the future that will be rewarding to you?

Are you insecure or nervous about an aspect of your job? What would happen if you delved into this area?

Think about the people around you. Is there something someone does that you think is valuable or unique? Have you told this person? Why or why not?

Reflect on a risk that you've taken. What did you learn from it?

Reflect on a mistake you've made. What did you learn from it? How does it help you in your life today?

UNLEARNING WHAT YOU THOUGHT WAS SO

Now this is a hard one! Why, if learning takes such energy, commitment, and resources, would anyone want to spend more time and energy in the "unlearning" process? The answer, of course, is to grow. This kind of "unlearning" growth is particularly difficult because it demands that the individual let go. As Peter Vaill said in *Learning as a Way of Being,* "We do not need competency skills for this life. We need incompetency skills, the skills of being effective beginners."

Consider your experience with "unlearning" and reflect on the following questions:

When have you had to back up and relearn something you believed as true? How did this happen?

What are some coping mechanisms you used or can use to overcome the feelings of inadequacy that come with unlearning?

What are some behaviors individuals can develop to ensure that they are learning all they can, even in familiar environments?

How can being open to new learnings help in situations where diversity presents itself?

PAIN IS A GREAT TEACHER

Why is it that the most painful experiences in our lives often lead to the most significant lessons? Each story in this section brought pain in some form to the writer. Yet each person was able to look past the pain and learn from the experience. What if he or she hadn't stopped to reflect? What would have been missed? R. L. Stine has a wonderful way of looking at the learning that is always inside the pain: "Sometimes when you least expect it, LIFE gives you a big ol' sock in the nose. Not to worry. With time, pain will pass, and from it you will have gained experience, which gives you information, which gives you objectivity, which gives you wisdom, which gives you truth, which gives you freedom from having to get a sock in the nose again."

Consider the following questions as you reflect on your own painful experiences:

Do you believe that pain presents opportunity? Why or why not?

What are some ways in which you resolve a painful experience? What other experiences stimulate us to change? When do we move out of our status quo?

Sometimes we learn the same lesson over and over. What is one lesson you seem to be stuck on?

Sometimes people point to specific events in their lives and say, "If it weren't for [fill in the blank], I would not be where I am today." What key moments in your life could you point to in this way?

MENTORS MATTER

People constantly influence our lives. They reach, direct, support, and nurture us. The mentors or helpers in these stories ranged from traditional teachers to unlikely sources of influence. Clearly, individuals can be mentors without knowing that they are playing this role. The power of our mentors may not lie in a particular model they give us, but may be in their capacity to wake us up to an important lesson, the significance of which we realize only later. And we are often unaware of the mentoring that could be ours simply for the asking! All around us are opportunities to mentor others and receive gifts from those who fill our lives. Think about your willingness and capacity to mentor others, as well as your openness to having others mentor you.

Consider the following questions in your exploration:

How have mentors contributed to your learning?

Who have your mentors been?

How did you find your mentor, or how did your mentor find you?

How have you contributed to someone else's learning?

In what ways could you mentor others around you?

What did you learn from being a mentor?

Who was your most effective mentor? Why?

What behaviors and attitudes are necessary for a learner to get the most out of a mentor?

CONFERENCE ROOM, BOARDROOM, HOMEROOM

This book was created not simply as an anthology of interesting bedtime stories from professionals in the teaching and consulting fields. The stories have been collected and shared because of a passion and belief in the power of personal experience as captured in the form of a story. These stories are meant to share knowledge and wisdom, and most important, to inspire you to explore and bring to life your own experiences.

If the stories in this book are to be more than just interesting reading, they must be taken into the classroom and into the meeting rooms of organizations of all sizes and shapes. The appendix at the end of the book is intended to help you take that step. The ideas the stories spark need to be positioned and presented by skilled facilitators who are interested in making the workplace a forum for the exploration of individual differences and for the sharing of individual experiences, all of which build the capacity of a learning organization.

The authors hope you will use these stories to create the kind of dialogue and discussion that usually does not take place in our organizations. Through sharing our stories, we begin to see the richness of our diversity and the value in each person with whom we work. Creating space for these conversations can only add meaningfulness and depth to the places in which we work.

The editors of this book would love to know which of these questions or exercises proved most useful, or what you may have done to bring the pages of this book to life. As you reflect upon the stories and questions in this book, we would love to have you send your thoughts to LearningJourneys@KGCnet.com.

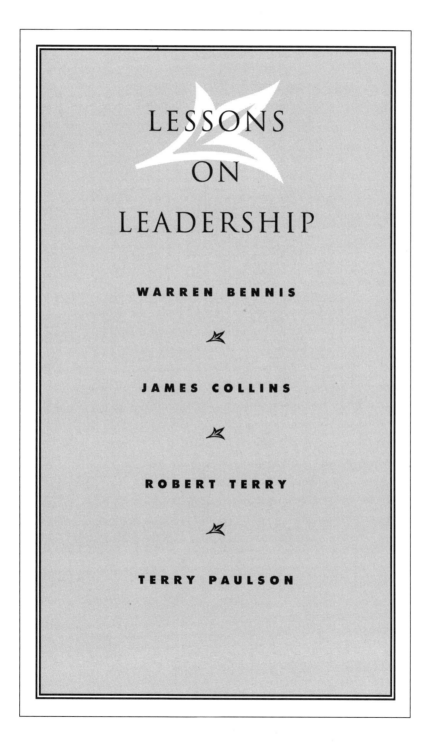

LESSONS
ON
LEADERSHIP

WARREN BENNIS

JAMES COLLINS

ROBERT TERRY

TERRY PAULSON

1

WARREN BENNIS

Warren Bennis is distinguished professor of business administration and founding chairman of the Leadership Institute at the University of Southern California. He has been observing and writing about leaders and managers for more than five decades. His many books include the best-selling Leaders *and* On Becoming a Leader, *and the Pulitzer Prize–nominated* An Invented Life, *as well as* Organizing Genius, Managing People Is Like Herding Cats, *and* Old Dogs, New Tricks. *Bennis has served on the faculties of Massachusetts Institute of Technology's Sloan School of Management, Harvard University, and Boston University, and he has been executive vice president of the State University of New York at Buffalo and president of the University of Cincinnati.*

Write Your Own Life

We all face the great challenge to discover our native abilities and to invent and reinvent ourselves throughout life. I believe in self-invention as an exercise of the imagination. It is how we get to know ourselves. People who can't invent and reinvent themselves must be content with borrowed postures, secondhand ideas, and fitting in instead of standing out. Inventing oneself is the opposite of accepting the roles we were brought up to play.

To be authentic is literally to be your own author (the words derive from the same Greek root), to discover your native energies and desires, and then to find your own way of acting on them. When you do that, you are not existing simply to live up to an image posited by the culture, family tradition, or some other authority. When you write your own life, you are playing the game that is natural for you to play. You are keeping covenant with your own promise.

MY OWN ROOTS

The landscape of my childhood was very like a Beckett stage set: barren, meager, endless. A little boy waited there for someone who might not, probably would not, show up. There were walk-ons occasionally: twin brothers, ten years my senior; a father who worked eighteen hours a day (when he took off his shoes and soiled socks, the ring of dirt around his ankles had to be scrubbed off with a stiff-bristled brush); and a mother who liked vaudeville and played mah-jongg with her friends when she wasn't helping my father eke out an existence.

I was withdrawn, sullen, detached, removed from hope or desire, and probably depressed—"mopey," my father called it. I was also left pretty much alone. I had no close friends. I can't remember how I spent my time, except I know that I made up improved versions of my life that ran like twenty-four-hour newsreels in my mind.

I didn't much like school, and I barely remember my teachers, except for Miss Shirer. I liked Miss Shirer enormously. She taught the eighth grade, and she was almost famous because her older brother, William Shirer, was broadcasting from Berlin on CBS. I leaned into the radio whenever Shirer was on. That he was anti-Hitler was thrilling to a kid who, in 1938, often felt like the only Jew in Westwood, New Jersey, a town that richly deserved its reputation as a major stronghold of the German Bund.

On one momentous occasion, Miss Shirer asked us to spend about ten minutes telling the class about our favorite hobby. I panicked. After all, I liked Miss Shirer a lot, but the truth was that I didn't have anything remotely like a favorite hobby. My efforts to develop recreational interests like those of the other guys had failed miserably. I was mediocre at sports. I was bored with collecting stamps. I was too clumsy to tie dry flies, too nervous to hunt, and too maladroit to build model airplanes out of balsa wood. What I finally decided to do, in a moment of desperate inspiration, was to bring in a box full of shoe polish, different colors and shades in cans and bottles, since the only palpable physical activity I regularly engaged in was shining the family shoes.

And so, when it was my turn in the spotlight, I revealed the arcane nature of a new art form. I described in loving detail the nuances of my palette (I was especially good on the subtle differences between oxblood and maroon). I discoursed on the form and function of the various appliances needed to achieve an impressive tone and sheen. I argued both sides of the debate on solid versus liquid wax and wrapped it all up with a spirited disquisition on the multiple virtues of neat's-foot oil. It was a remarkable performance, if only because it was, from start to finish, an act of pure imagination. I could tell from her smile that Miss Shirer thought it was terrific. Even the class seemed impressed in a stupefied way. And there, in a flourish of brushes and shoe polish, a new Warren Bennis was born.

ARMY AND SCHOOL

When I graduated from high school into the army during World War II (1943–1947), I saw firsthand the consequences of good and bad leadership in the simplest and starkest terms—morale, tank support that would or would not be where it was supposed to be, wounds, and body counts. The army was the first organization I was to observe close-up and in depth. And although I have been in more pleasant classrooms, it was an excellent place to study such organizational realities as the effects of command-and-control leadership and the paralyzing impact of institutional bureaucracy. The army also taught me the value of being organized.

Once out of the army, I attended Antioch College (1947–1951), where I learned to have opinions. That may not sound very important, but it amounted to a personal paradigm shift. What freedom, what liberation it was to have opinions. Having opinions was, at least for me, tantamount to developing a personal identity.

To get through the Ph.D. program at MIT (1951–1956), I began to memorize and mimic. I imitated my professors and the brightest of my fellow graduate students. For roughly two years, I lip-synched what I heard. Eventually, the words I formed on my lips came more naturally, but I often wondered whether I was kidding myself.

From 1955 to 1971, I made stops in Bethel, Maine, where everyone was buzzing over Kurt Lewin's T-groups; Boston University, where I taught psychology and underwent psychoanalysis; and SUNY Buffalo, where I learned that unless a vision is sustained by action, it quickly turns to ashes.

UNIVERSITY PRESIDENT

As president of the University of Cincinnati (1971 to 1978), I finally realized that my principal role model would have to be me. I decided that the kind of university president I wanted to be was one who led, not managed. That's an important difference. Many an institution is well managed yet poorly led. The staff may excel in the ability to handle all the daily routines, yet they never ask whether the routine should be engaged in the first place.

My entrapment in minutiae made me realize another thing: People were following the old army game. They did not want to take responsibility for the decisions they needed to make. "Let's push up the tough ones" had become the motto. As a result, everybody was dumping his or her "wet babies" (as old hands at the State Department called them) on my desk. I decided then and there that my highest priority was to create an "executive constellation" to run the office of the president. The sole requirements for inclusion in the group were that the individual needed to know more than I did about his or her area of competence and had to be willing to take care of daily matters without referring them back to me. I was going to make the time to lead.

I realized that I had been doing what so many leaders do. I was trying to be everything to the organization: father, fixer, policeman, ombudsman, rabbi, therapist, and banker. As a CEO who was similarly afflicted put it to me later, "If I'm walking on the shop floor and see a leak in the dike, I have to stick my finger in." Trying to be everything to everyone was diverting me from real leadership. It was burning me out. And perhaps worst of all, it was denying all the potential leaders under me the chance to learn and prove themselves.

Things got better after that, although I never came close to the ideal. As I look back at my experience at UC, I compare it with my psychoanalysis: I wouldn't have missed it for the world, and I would never go through it again. In becoming a leader I learned a number of important things about both leadership and myself. As Sophocles observes in *Antigone,* "But hard it is to learn the mind of any mortal, or the heart, 'til he be tried in chief authority. Power shows the man."

Having executive power showed me some personal truths. First, I was, as the song says, "Looking for love in all the wrong places." Intellectually, I knew that leaders can't, and shouldn't, count on being loved. But I seriously underestimated the emotional impact of angry constituents. I believed the false dream that people would love me if only they really got to know me.

Anyone in authority is to some extent the hostage of how others perceive him or her. The perceptions of other people can be a prison. For the first time I began to understand what it must be like to be the victim of prejudice, to be helpless in the steel embrace of how other people see you. People impute motives to their leaders, love or hate them, seek them out or avoid them, and idolize or demonize them, independent of what the leaders do or who they are. Ironically, at the very time I had the most power, I felt the greatest sense of powerlessness.

And I realized an important personal truth. I was never going to be completely happy with positional power, the only kind of power an organization can bestow. What I really wanted was personal power, influence based on voice.

THE AUTUMN OF MY DAYS

I am now in my twentieth year at USC, my longest continuous tenure at any institution. In many ways it has been the happiest period of my life. USC has provided me with exactly the right social architecture to do what seems most important to me now: teaching in the broadest sense.

At USC I have the leisure to consolidate what I've learned about self-invention, about the importance of organization, about the nature of change, and about the nature of leadership, as well as to find ways to communicate those lessons. Erik Erikson talks about an eight-stage process of human development. I think I have entered Erikson's seventh stage, the generative one, in which self-absorption gives way to an altruistic surrender to the next generation. Although writing is my greatest joy, I also take enormous pleasure in people-growing, in watching others bloom, in mentoring as I was mentored.

What I have discovered is that the need to reinvent oneself, to "compose a life," as Mary Catherine Bateson puts it, is ongoing. Just a few years ago my closest friend, Sam Jaffe, who died this year at ninety-eight (and who in his fifties was the Academy Award–winning producer of *Born Free*), and I took a summer course on Dickens at Trinity Hall, Cambridge. Sam, who tried to buy the film rights to a book I had given him, continued in his nineties to scrimmage in the notoriously competitive subculture of Hollywood. He gave me hope.

I find that I have acquired a new set of priorities. Some of the old agonies have simply disappeared. I have no doubt that my three children are more important than anything else in my life. Having achieved a certain level of worldly success, I need hardly think about it anymore. Gentler virtues seem terribly important now. I strive to be generous and productive. I would hope to be thought of as a decent and creative man.

I think Miss Shirer would be proud.

QUESTIONS

⚔ *What do you think are your native abilities?*

⚔ *How are you currently using those abilities, and how would you like to use them in the future?*

⚔ *Are you living a life that would make a former teacher, parent, or coach proud of you?*

2 JAMES COLLINS

James Collins is a student and teacher of senior executives and CEOs at enduring great companies. He began his research and teaching career on the faculty at Stanford Graduate School of Business. In 1995, he founded a management laboratory in Boulder, Colorado, where he now conducts multiyear research projects and works with executives from the private, public, and social sectors. Collins has coauthored three books, including the classic Built to Last *(on the* Business Week *best-seller list for nearly five years). Currently, he is completing his new book,* Good to Great, *to be published by HarperCollins. For a comprehensive list of the books and artlicles he has published, go to www.jimcollins.com. Collins can be reached at jcc512@aol.com.*

The Learning Executive

How would your day be different if you organized your time, energy, and resources primarily around the objective of learning, instead of around performance? For many people, their daily activities—what they do and how they go about doing it—

Copyright ©1997 by Jim Collins. This article first appeared in *Inc.,* August 1997.

would be dramatically changed. Indeed, despite all the buzz around the concept of the "learning organization," I'm struck by how few people seem to have embraced the idea of being a true learning person.

This came home to me during an interview with a television producer developing a documentary on Sam Walton. After about forty-five minutes, she asked if I had anything else to add, indicating the end of the interview. "No," I said, "but I'd like to ask you some questions." She paused, obviously not prepared for my request, and then gave an uncertain, "Okay." For the next fifteen minutes, I had the great pleasure of asking her questions about what she had learned in her research. The producer had no background in business—having done most of her documentaries on historical figures like Stalin and Mozart—so I thought she might have a fresh and illuminating perspective. She did, and I learned some new information and gained new insights about one of my favorite subjects.

"That's the first time that's ever happened to me," she said. "I interview professors and experts all the time, but I've never had one turn the tables and begin asking me questions. At first I was taken aback—surprised really—but it's refreshing to see that experts can still learn."

Stop and think about that for a minute. Here's a bright television producer who spends her life delving into specific subjects— a walking treasure trove of knowledge—and people whose profession is to continually learn don't pause to take the opportunity to expand their expertise further by talking with her. They act as knowers rather than learners, which, incidentally, is just the opposite of what Sam Walton did.

Walton viewed himself not as a definitive expert on retailing but as a lifelong student of his craft, always asking questions and taking every opportunity to learn. A Brazilian businessman once told me that of ten U.S. retailing CEOs he wrote to asking for an appointment after he'd purchased a discount retailing chain in

South America, only Walton said yes. "We didn't know much about retailing, so we wanted to talk to executives who knew the business," he explained. "Most didn't bother to reply. Sam said, 'Sure, come on up.' Only later did I realize he was as interested in learning from us as we were in learning from him; he pummeled us with questions about Brazil. Later, we launched a joint venture with Wal-Mart in South America."

Becoming a learning person certainly involves responding to every situation with learning in mind, as Walton did. But it involves more than that; it requires setting explicit learning objectives. Look at your personal list of long-term objectives, your midterm objectives, and your current to-do list. How many items fall into the performance genre and how many fall into the learning genre? How many begin with the structure "My objective is to learn X," rather than "My objective is to accomplish Y"? Most people operate off of to-do lists. They're a useful mechanism for getting things done. A true learning person also has a "to-learn" list, and the items on that list carry at least as much weight in how one organizes his or her time as the to-do list.

Granite Rock, in Watsonville, California, one of the few authentic learning organizations, has institutionalized this idea by replacing performance goals for individuals with learning goals. The stone, concrete, and asphalt supplier makes the shift explicit by asking each employee to set his or her annual objectives in the format "Learn _____ so that I can _____."

Learning people also develop explicit learning mechanisms, such as "learning logs" or formal "autopsies"—time explicitly set aside to discuss or reflect on events and extract the maximum knowledge and understanding from them. Such people plant seeds of learning that will flower later. One prominent thinker I spent a day with ended our discussion with the statement, "I have a small consulting fee: you must keep me informed as to your learning and progress." Every six months or so I send him a letter, and I imagine he gets dozens of such learning letters a year. I've also found the mechanism of a learning notebook to be useful; in it I keep track of my learning and observations about life, work, myself, or whatever seems interesting, much the same way a scientist keeps a lab book on any subject of inquiry. It's a powerful mechanism for identifying not only learning but also the activities where I'm not learning (which I then unplug or redesign).

I'm not yet as much of a learning person as I'd like to be. Like most Americans, I'm driven largely by an urge to perform, accomplish, achieve, and get things done. Yet as I begin to consciously shift to filtering everything through a learning lens, I find both dramatic and subtle differences in the way I do things and how I spend my time. With a "get things done" lens, I'll leave a voicemail; with a learning lens, I'll seek a real-time phone call during which I can ask questions and learn from conversation. With a performance lens, I'll try to impress the interviewer with my knowledge; with a learning lens, I'll ask her questions. Even mundane activities like washing dishes, shaving, and walking through airports can be transformed by carrying a portable tape player and listening to unabridged books on tape.

John W. Gardner, author of the classic book *Self-Renewal: The Individual and Innovative Society* (and a man who keeps an active learning and teaching schedule well into his 80s), captured the spirit of the learning person with his admonition "Don't set out in life to be an interesting person; set out to be an interested person." Learning people, of which Gardner is a prime example, learn till the day they die, not because learning will "get them somewhere," but because they see learning as part of the reason for living. When asked for an economic justification for learning, they find the question as odd as being asked for a financial justification for breathing. The link between learning and performance is self-evident, but for a true learning person (or organization, for that matter), performance is not the ultimate why of learning. Learning is the why of learning. And until we grasp that fact and organize accordingly, we will not—indeed cannot—build the elusive learning organization.

QUESTIONS

- ✍ *How would your life be different if you organized your time, energy, and resources around the objective of learning, rather than around performance?*

- ✍ *If you look at your personal list of long-term, midterm, and short-term objectives, how many items fall into the performance genre and how many into the learning genre?*

- ✍ *Does your "to learn" list carry at least as much weight as your to-do list?*

3

ROBERT TERRY

*Dr. Robert Terry is president of the Terry Group. He is
an internationally recognized leadership educator and
senior executive adviser. For more than a decade he has
been senior fellow and director of the Reflective Leadership Center at the Humphrey Institute of Public Affairs
at the University of Minnesota. Terry is the author of
two books and is currently working on a third, entitled*
Zone Leadership: Mapping the World for Authentic
Action. *A much-in-demand speaker and seminar leader,
he has received several awards for outstanding teaching
and leadership.*

We Are Always Challenged
to Be Authentic

A sea anchor floats behind a vessel to prevent drifting or
to maintain a heading into the wind. It goes with you; it doesn't
lock you into place but rather provides a kind of stability in the
midst of change. This story is about the value of sacred texts as sea
anchors for the journey.

In 1967, I finished my Ph.D. at the University of Chicago and decided to join the Detroit Industrial Mission (DIM). My dissertation had been on DIM, an ecumenical group working on human value questions in business. The group had invited me to join the staff, and I moved to Detroit on July 1. Just three weeks later the city was embroiled in rebellion, and I was soon caught up in great causes I could be passionate about. This began a very transformative time in my life, a time when I began to learn that there would always be causes I could and would commit myself to, but there was so much more I needed to learn about life itself.

One of the members of the staff at DIM was a man named Jim Campbell. Jim was a Presbyterian minister who had worked on the assembly line at Cadillac for five years to try to figure out how organizations work. He was a wonderful person and quite my opposite in many ways. We had very different styles and very different approaches, yet we formed a marvelous bond. Over time, his family and mine became very close. We began spending Thanksgivings and Christmases together. Eventually we had vacation cottages side by side on a lake in Canada, and we'd gather there as families every summer.

After several years, I left DIM and was out on my own, yet Jim and I maintained a close friendship. On Christmas Eve day in 1981, Jim and I were working on a project. Jim had complained of a swelling in his jaw and had an appointment with his dentist later that day to check it out. When I called his home in the evening, one of his three young daughters answered the phone. She was crying, and she said, "Dad has leukemia, and he wants you to do his funeral."

I had never experienced the death of a peer, much less of a friend. I had performed a funeral for my grandmother and another for a small child I hadn't actually known. But none of my friends had died, and certainly none had ever told me he was dying. I was stunned.

I called my pastor and said, "How do you deal with someone who is dying? I have no idea. I didn't learn about this in seminary, or else it didn't sink in."

"Well," he said, "the only thing I can tell you is to be available when he wants you to be available—not when you want to be available."

I took his advice seriously. I thought, "How in the world am I going to be available? I'm a consultant. I'm always traveling. How am I going to be available to him?"

I decided I would call him on the phone every day when he was in the hospital. And if I was in town, I'd go see him. He was in the hospital 178 days.

We talked on the phone for thirty seconds or for an hour; it was always Jim's decision how long we talked. We talked through his living and dying, and my living and dying, and the funeral. Once he said, "Now when you do the funeral, don't be maudlin!" And I said, "I'll be maudlin if I want to, you so-and-so. You're the one who's dying." Talking at this level was profound for me, because I hadn't worked through my own fears about dying. And I'd certainly never had anybody who was dying describe the process and what it means. It was profoundly challenging.

During that time, I learned that I'd been accepted to the post of director of the Reflective Leadership Center at the Humphrey Institute. Jim was the first person I called with the news. It was a bittersweet call because I was excited about new possibilities while he had just come out of remission for the second time. He had no confidence—nor did I—that he would go into remission again. His days seemed numbered.

I moved to Minneapolis to start my new job, and the first piece of mail waiting for me was a letter from Jim, expressing concern about me. This letter is my sacred text, my anchor. The letter read, in part:

Dear Bob:

I felt sad when you left yesterday and yet a little jealous of all the new things and the excitement ahead of you, but basically I'm glad you have the position. It's what you want and need. . . .

I'll miss you, my buddy. I'm trusting great distance won't mean real distance. With a lump in my throat and eyes a bit wet, I long for yet more days together on Half Moon [our lake in Canada] . . . a project or two and just enjoying ourselves.

I hope I make it. I hope you can get there despite all the new pressures . . . I hope a lot of things and wonder if they'll possibly be. . . .

Like when a minister is ordained, I feel I should give you a "charge" in your new job, but doubt if I have much wisdom for you. One thing is to keep your own fertile mind fine-tuned even as you seek to expand the minds of the "leaders." Another is, amid all of the big shots you'll be hobnobbing with, not to forget the little people around you at the institute who keep things going and do the shit work. . . .

And then Jim closed the letter with some personal comments.

I have this letter framed, and it's on my desk at all times. This is a great gift to me, this letter. It's a sea anchor that gives me calm. All these years later, it still strikes me as remarkable that there Jim was worrying about me and writing a letter giving me words of wisdom while I was so preoccupied with worry about him. From his own illness he was still able to reach out and express love for someone else, which was his essence. That was a profound lesson for me. It's easy to become a victim, but it takes a lot of courage to face the world and own it and still move in the midst of it.

This is where I learned a lot about leadership. Leadership is more about who you are as a human being than what you do for a living. It's more about being than doing. If we don't have deep soul and a deep sense of ourselves as we engage with the world, leadership becomes manipulative: How can I get you to do what I want you to do and have you feel good about it?

To me, the profound challenge in leadership is authenticity— being true and real in ourselves, in our relationships, and in the world. That's what Jim invited me to do. Don't forget the little people. Don't get caught up with the big shots. Everybody has truth, everybody has insight, and everybody has a contribution to make.

I've learned that if I forget the little people and get caught up in the arrogance of working with the power players, then I'm off track. My authenticity is compromised, and I don't have a clue what's going on. Jim's reminder is a profound anchor, because we are always challenged to be authentic.

Prior to my relationship with Jim, I had always been into causes, particularly into fighting racism. After Jim died, I pondered my causes and what they meant to me. I made a deep shift from focusing on causes to focusing on relationships. Today I'm still committed to causes, but now I work harder on the intimacy of relationships. What I learned from Jim and want to share with others is that authentic relationships are the essence of life.

As you build the quality of authenticity—authentic relationships for the long term—the world unfolds in spectacular ways. If we're open and we're strong in our convictions, the world invites us to go to some interesting and unexpected places. But to go there with somebody and not all alone is to be supported and encouraged. That's what I learned from Jim. His letter to me has translated into my gift to others.

QUESTIONS

⚔ *How do you nurture authenticity in your relationships?*

⚔ *What is your sacred text? What is true and constant for you?*

⚔ *What's the story around it? Do you share it with others?*

⚔ *What is your anchor?*

4 TERRY PAULSON

Terry Paulson, Ph.D., is a licensed psychologist, the 1998–99 president of the National Speakers Association, and author of They Shoot Managers Don't They? *and* 50 Tips for Speaking Like a Pro. *As a speaker and trainer for such organizations as Sears, IBM, American Medical Association, Merck, and 3M, he helps leaders and teams make changes.* Business Digest *calls him "the Will Rogers of management consultants." In addition to once having been a lab technician truck driver at the Stanford Linear Accelerator, Terry was chosen "Scooper of the Month" by Baskin-Robbins in May 1964.*

The Power of Listening

When I was seventeen, I helped build the mile-long electron microscope at the Stanford Linear Accelerator in Palo Alto, California. My job title that summer was "lab technician" (probably for funding purposes), but I drove a truck. I worked hard for three months as part of an eight-man construction team. This was my first big job, and I was proud to be part of the team. I was open to all the possibilities that venturing into the real world of work can conjure up. I had previously spent some time working on a family farm in Illinois and had also picked apricots by the hour, but now I had an actual job title, and I was paid well enough that I could afford to go out. That was progress.

As with most memorable events, it is the people, not the work, that we remember. That summer was no exception. I got to meet Jack Nichols, the best supervisor I've ever met. Long before anyone talked about "empowering" leadership or related fads, Jack lived empowerment. Jack had a statement on his wall that I will never forget. I'm not sure who said it first, but since it was on Jack's wall, I will give him the credit. The sign read: "Every person I work with knows something better than I. My job is to listen long enough to find it and use it."

Jack literally walked his talk. Every week he took a fifteen-minute walk with each of his direct subordinates. Even as his only summer employee, I was expected to join him for a walk on the project every Friday. What impressed me most was that during our walks he seldom did much talking; Jack preferred to invest his time in listening. And it was the questions he repeatedly asked that fostered a pivotal emotional learning experience in my young life.

The question that had the biggest impact on me was the first question he asked. Jack liked to get right to the point. His words hung in the air as we walked: "Terry, you've been working here a week; what's working for you?" Of all the questions he could ask, he had to pick one I had no ready answer for. You don't ask teens what is working for them! You ask them, How is it going in school? Are you scoring any touchdowns? and even, Are you on drugs? I was usually quick with good answers, but this one took me more than a few uncomfortable moments of searching for anything that would work. I finally replied tentatively, "I know the equipment is very sensitive, so the guys have taught me how to load the truck. That's been working." He was glad I was learning from the team, but his next sentence was a surprise. He said thoughtfully, "When I first met you, Terry, I knew that there was something special about you. In fact, I expect to learn something from you this summer. I'm going to ask you this question every Friday."

I couldn't believe his words! Had this man forgotten what it was like to be a teenager? I, like other teens, did what adults told me to do. I was good at taking tests and giving back the answers the adults told me to learn. Didn't he know that the guys I was working with weren't going to give me a new idea to share with him every week? This guy seemed to respect me enough to ask me for my ideas. He had to be crazy! I was sure that if he could just talk to my mother, she would confirm that I didn't know anything of value. She might even write me an excuse note!

Jack ruined my summer! I had to think, not just do a job. But like any good student, I went to the only authority model I knew—teachers. I had done well in school by learning how teachers gave tests. I studied everything for the first test, but once I had that test, I could learn the teacher's test paradigm. If the tests covered only class notes, I just scanned the text and focused my study on the notes. Jack helped me learn an important lesson about leadership that summer. Jack taught me that, just like teachers, leaders are known by the questions they consistently ask. Jack's question was, What's working for you? He didn't give me the answer; he wanted me to come up with my own. I had to think differently. Soon my best day was always Thursday. If nothing had worked by Thursday, I had a mission. Something had to work, because my walk was Friday. I always had something to share on Friday, and Jack always listened.

In retrospect, I can see that Jack knew how to get the best out of his team. He was not particularly charismatic, but he came alive as a listener. He was more excited about my ideas than he was about his own. He would ask questions to expand my thinking. He would nod his approval, even encourage me to take it further. I'm sure some of my ideas were a bit bizarre, but he always treated them with thoughtful dignity.

Twice that summer he asked me if I would mind if he shared my idea with the team at the staff meeting. I agreed, at the same time trying to hide my excitement behind an appropriate amount of macho indifference. The first time, I thought he had forgotten my idea. Then, halfway through the staff meeting, he said, "Terry came up with something the other day. In fact, he did such a good job of explaining it to me, Terry, why don't you tell the men what you told me?"

My heart raced. Panic! No, this is not good! I'm a kid; these people are old—thirty or thirty-one! But Jack's eyes and warm smile settled me. I looked only at him as I shared my idea. We changed procedures twice that summer as a result of my input. I felt special, but it did not make me special. It did, however, make Jack very special as a leader because he did the same for each member of the team. As he walked me to the car on my last day that summer, he said, "Terry, if you ever need a job, you come back. You made a difference here." I went into my senior year of high school on a high. I had made a difference in the real world. I had also inherited a mentor and heart hero who to this day helps guide me in finding what works.

Our world of work tends to focus on problems. The questions leaders ask often reflect that preoccupation—What's wrong? Got any problems? What, no problems? Then get back to work! Jack lived his leadership by helping his team look for opportunities. He didn't push his team; he helped us soar on the wings of our own ideas. Both as a leader and as a professional speaker and trainer, I try to reflect that same focus. Life in this constantly changing world is like a moving vehicle with no brakes. There is no off switch, no reverse, and no easy off-ramp. That is why the rearview mirror is smaller than your front window. Too many people live in the rearview mirror, preoccupied with problems that are already over. Jack helped me focus on what I could make happen over the next horizon, and I've been enjoying the journey ever since.

QUESTIONS

*   *As a leader, you are known by the questions you consistently ask. Okay, you knew I was going to ask: What's working for you?*

*   *What role can you play in mentoring others to see the contributions they can make?*

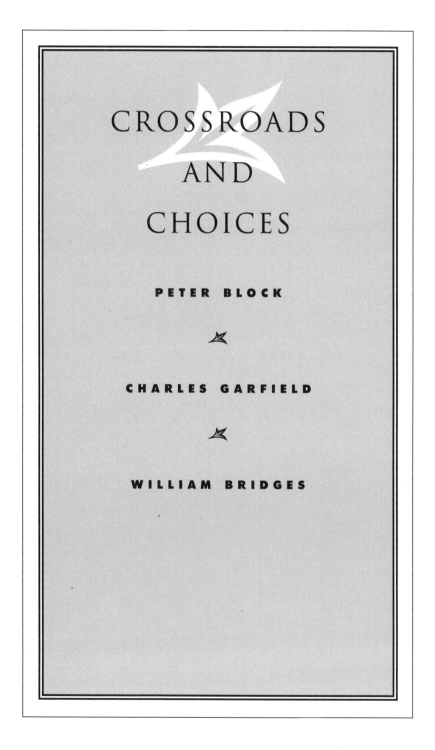

CROSSROADS
AND
CHOICES

PETER BLOCK

CHARLES GARFIELD

WILLIAM BRIDGES

5   PETER BLOCK

*Peter Block is an author, consultant, and speaker who
helped spark the interest in empowerment and whose
work now centers on ways to bring service and accountability to organizations and communities. He founded
the consulting firm Block Petrella Weisbord in 1968 and
in 1980 began Designed Learning. Block is on the board
of directors of the Association for Quality and Participation and has joined with AQP to create the School for
Managing and Leading Change. He is the author of three
best-selling books:* Flawless Consulting, The Empowered Manager, *and* Stewardship: Choosing Service
Over Self-Interest. *Block's office is in Connecticut. He
can be reached at (860) 572-0346 or pbi@att.net.*

Everything Counts

I can't think of anything that has had an impact on my life
that hasn't changed my work, and I can't think of anything significant that has happened in my work that hasn't changed my
life. Personal changes, changes in thinking, and changes in practice are all one and the same. There have been several events in my
work that caused my thinking to shift in a major way.

I first started in organization development in my late twenties working with T-groups. For almost five years I worked under the belief that the point was to always get it right. I believed that when I spoke, I should speak what was true and well thought out, and when I did my work, I should have a clear goal in mind. I was anxious and ambitious, and I wanted to be somebody.

After leading groups for a number of years, I began to participate in weekend Gestalt workshops. Up to that point, I had focused on being a good trainer, consultant, father, husband, and neighbor. I was meeting the external requirements of what the world expected of me and of what I expected of myself. From Gestalt work, I got the expression "Who you are is everything." What defines you as a person is not what you do, what you did, or how you present yourself. I came to believe that what defines a people is their capacity to understand and give expression to their own experience. My focus switched from viewing life on the basis of accomplishment to that of experience.

This learning redefined how I worked. Instead of asking people, "What would constitute an agreement?" or, "How do we resolve this issue?" I would ask them questions about what they were experiencing. I discovered that resolution of conflict comes from people being able to express their own feelings and their own needs in the face of another. Making agreements and setting goals without building upon the feelings of the parties involved is empty, because it does not consider the vulnerabilities of our own humanity. What counts is an individual's capacity to express or state who he or she is, not so much the ability to set and reach a specific goal.

The second major turning point occurred when I was thirty-six. I read Tim Gallwey's *Inner Game of Tennis.* Using the game of tennis as a metaphor, Gallwey offered stunning insights about performing and learning. His basic stance is that awareness, body awareness in the case of tennis, is the antidote to self-doubt and self-judgment. This turned on a light bulb in my brain and gave me a way to become more connected to the world and to myself.

I was also greatly affected by his notion that in terms of our spiritual and philosophical lives, we have within us the wisdom to answer all our questions. Learning is a process of rediscovering what we already know. This caused me to question the purpose of skill training. Why do we prescribe behavior and ask people to practice, copy, and imitate? Doesn't this demean the human spirit and destroy what is part of the individual? To prescribe to people what they should learn or how they should perform is to keep them from truly learning.

For example, I used to hate talking in front of people. I'm an introvert. I would fight myself when I gave a presentation. I tried hard to be dynamic and charismatic, to fulfill the image of the ideal presenter that was in my head. Finally I said, "To hell with it. I'm never going to be a good speaker. Why don't I just stand up and say something?" And as a result I became a good presenter. I stopped trying so hard. I understood that my anxiety was about finding my own voice. It was a sign of being alive, so get on with it.

The third life-changing event occurred when I was forty. I was in Stockholm running an Inner Game of Tennis clinic, and I happened to go to a lecture by Peter Koestenbaum. Peter, a professor of philosophy, talked about a deep part of the structure of life in which each person has to deal with fundamental issues, such as purpose, destiny, aloneness, and mortality—issues I had never taken seriously. In an audience of 300 I sat paralyzed. I don't know if half of what he said even registered, but just the idea that destiny and purpose were everybody's issue stunned me.

I left Peter's lecture with the simple wish that he would not visit my workshop to witness the superficiality and shallowness that would be visible for all to see. Luckily he came in late, and afterward I told him how touched I was by what he had said. I asked him if I could visit him and told him I needed help in understanding what he was talking about.

I visited Peter at his home in San Jose and explained to him that about every seven years, my life seems to dissemble and I find myself having to start over again. In response to this, Peter asked me, "What is your destiny?" I replied that I didn't know. The questions of choosing greatness and purpose, as well as the fact that reaffirming your life mattered, were huge issues for me. I attended every lecture of his I could, and every time I was in California I would visit him. It was another ten years before I understood what he was talking about.

Peter's influence helped me create all the work I did with empowerment. I became a translator of Peter's ideas into the workplace. There are questions that are still unanswered, but the important point is that I know they are there. The question of "calling" is part of that. Each of us needs to find out what we're here for and pursue it. We each have a vision of greatness, whether or not we want to accept it.

People ask me sometimes what impact I've had on people over the last thirty years. The answer is none. Maybe at my best I've touched other people's lives as Gestalt workshops, Tim Gallwey, and Peter Koestenbaum have touched mine, but I don't give them credit for my life. They have added tremendous value. Others give a gift, but in the end each of us chooses and is responsible for our own life.

QUESTIONS

↗ *What courage is required at this point in our life?*

↗ *How do we reclaim the freedom we have so easily given away?*

6   CHARLES GARFIELD

Dr. Charles Garfield is author of the best-selling books
Peak Performers: The New Heroes of American
Business *and* Second to None: The Protective Power
of Putting People First. *CEO of the Charles Garfield
Group in Oakland, California, he is recognized as one
of America's most accomplished speakers on individual,
team, and organizational performance.*

The Dancing Toll Taker

If you have ever gone through a tollbooth, you know that
your relationship to the person in the booth is not the most intimate you'll ever have. It is one of life's frequent non-encounters:
You hand over some money; you might get change; you drive off.

I have been through every one of the seventeen tollbooths on
the Oakland–San Francisco Bay Bridge on thousands of occasions,

and I never had an exchange with a toll taker that was worth remembering until late one morning in 1984.

I was headed for lunch in San Francisco as I drove toward one of the booths. I heard loud rock music. It sounded like a party or a Michael Jackson concert. I looked around—no other cars with their windows open, no sound trucks. I looked at the tollbooth. Inside it, a man was dancing.

"What are you doing?" I asked.

"I'm having a party," he said.

"What about the rest of these people?" I looked over at other booths; nothing moving there.

"They're not invited."

I had a dozen other questions for him, but somebody in a big hurry to get somewhere started punching his horn behind me. I drove off, but I made a note to myself: find this guy again. There's something in his eye that says there's magic in his tollbooth.

Months later I did find him again, still with the loud music, still having a party. Again I asked, "What are you doing?"

He said, "I remember you from the last time. I'm still dancing. I'm having the same party."

I said, "Look. What about the rest of these people?"

He said, "Stop. What do those look like to you?" He pointed down the row of tollbooths.

"They look like tollbooths."

"Noooo, imagination!"

I said, "Okay, I give up. What do they look like to you?"

He said, "Vertical coffins."

"What are you talking about?"

"I can prove it. At 8:30 every morning, live people get in. Then they die for eight hours. At 4:30, like Lazarus from the dead, they reemerge and go home. For eight hours, the brain is on hold, dead on the job. Going through the motions."

I was amazed. This guy had developed a philosophy, a mythology about his job. I could not help asking the next question: "Why is it different for you? You're having a good time."

He looked at me. "I knew you were going to ask that," he said. "I'm going to be a dancer someday." He pointed to the administration building. "My bosses are in there, and they're paying for my training."

Sixteen people dead on the job, and the seventeenth, in precisely the same situation, figures out a way to live. That man was having a party where you and I would probably not last three days. The boredom! He and I had lunch later, and he said, "I don't understand why anybody would think my job is boring. I have a corner office, glass on all sides. I can see the Golden Gate bridge, San Francisco, the Berkeley hills; half the Western world vacations here, and I just stroll in every day and practice dancing."

What is the essential skill that, when seventeen human beings walk into their offices and sixteen of them get vertical coffins, allows one of them to have a party? Mission. Purpose. Some people do the same jobs as everybody else but have an unusual sense of mission; they enjoy it, and they have the energy to achieve at high levels.

The dancing toll taker had been given no special jobs, no change in the conditions that limited life for everyone else in the booths. Yet he had found a mission, and thereby he had discovered the will and the way to use the conditions of his job to support his mission. He had found what Archimedes said he would need, along with his lever, to move the Earth: a place to stand.

He had found that place we might call a zone of peak performance, where he can align his personal mission with the specific demands of a job and the overall environment and objectives of an organization. It is a place for major productive impact, an optimal leverage point for one's abilities. I don't know if the toll taker has found the audience he was looking for, but I do know that when one observes peak performers long enough, it becomes increasingly clear that one of their major talents is finding such a place of personal power.

And why not? Their desire for a place to stand is based on keen appreciation of leverage, on the knowledge that it is from such a location that their mission has its best chance to succeed. When they have the abilities that a job requires and work in an environment that supports what they do, they encounter relatively little resistance.

Moreover, when a job provides the vehicle for accomplishing one's mission, when one's place to stand supports any task that may arise, one develops confidence in one's ability to complete the current mission and manage anything else that comes along.

What if the congruence is not there, and there is no solid place to stand, and you still have your job to do? Then it is tempting to force oneself, through superhuman acts of will, to overcome limitations in any of the three areas. We all know how hard it is to try to lift the weight with little leverage. People can be courageous and tenacious, and often do try to do the job even though they know they aren't in the right spot. People often know they are not positioned correctly for their best efforts, and it weakens their willingness to take a stand and their ability to manage what occurs along the way.

The place to stand suggests an opposite to the Peter Principle and its tart notion of people being promoted to their level of incompetence. I am talking about positioning ourselves for considerable competence, arriving at a place from which all things seem possible. And whether our specific road to achievement leads to Wall Street, Silicon Valley, or Damascus, we could, with tongue in cheek, call it the Paul Principle.

People who locate their place to stand like what they are doing. They feel a commitment to it. They feel themselves growing, learning, and experiencing through it. They have found not only their mission, but a firm standpoint, a situation, one might say an optimal context from which to make it happen. They see concrete results emerging from what they do. They, not just other people, recognize the contribution they are making.

QUESTIONS

⚔ *Are you one of the sixteen people dead on the job, or are you like the seventeenth toll taker?*

⚔ *Where is your place of personal power?*

⚔ *Do you recognize the contribution you are making? Do you feel yourself growing, learning, and experiencing through what you do?*

7

WILLIAM BRIDGES

William Bridges, president of William Bridges and Associates, speaks, writes, and conducts training programs on the subject of change and how organizations and individuals can deal with change successfully. He has written nine books, including Transitions, Managing Transition, *and* JobShift. *In 1993, the* Wall Street Journal *listed him as one of the top ten independent executive development presenters in the country. Bridges' clients have included AT&T, Intel, Hewlett-Packard, Amoco, and Procter & Gamble, as well as the Veterans Administration and the U.S. Department of Energy and the Department of Human Services. Educated in the humanities at Harvard, Columbia, and Brown universities, Bridges was a professor of American literature before changing careers at age forty. Bridges is also a past president of the Association for Humanistic Psychology.*

Living "As If"

When I was about forty years old, I was teaching literature at the college level. I had a sabbatical coming up, and during this sabbatical I spent a great deal of time researching the psychology of literature and how literature affects people. I had no idea what would come of this research, but I found it fascinating. When I tried to put my findings into words, the writing seemed very dead, and yet the subject was very alive to me. I didn't know why the ideas seemed to die when I wrote them down.

One day I was reading a section of what I had written to my wife. She said, "This is so academic." "I am an academic," I replied. "Give me a break." Then she explained what she meant: "You're talking a lot about what other people think. What do you think?" I gave a weasely answer, something like, "I'm just showing where my thoughts came from." But it rankled me to have her point out that I could talk about what other people said was so, but I never said what I thought was so.

The next day I started writing as though I knew what was true. But I had to write "as if," because at that time my mind was shaped by the academic, what-are-your-sources culture. As long as I could play a game with myself and say I'm only writing as if I know something, then I could playact my way into a kind of writing, which subsequently became speaking, that was more like bearing witness to a reality than it was like reporting on other people's perceptions of a reality.

I can't say how much of my life since that time has come straight from those days and how much I owe to acting as though my perceptions had some validity. At the time I was doing this, I was primarily teaching nineteenth-century U.S. writers, particularly Ralph Waldo Emerson, Henry David Thoreau, and Walt Whitman. All three were useful for demonstrating what I had learned, but a line from Emerson* stuck with me. He said, in effect, "Don't use quotations; tell me what you know."

I decided that I would take Emerson's point seriously. Emerson had been a minister and had resigned from that prestigious position. His wife died of tuberculosis not long after they were married, and in the period after her death, Emerson made a trip to Europe. Evidently, he just couldn't preach anymore. Emerson had had doubts about conventional Christianity, and his wife's death pulled out the last props from under him. While in Europe Emerson wrote in his journal, "I wonder if I have the courage to look at every part of the world in its relation to myself,

---

*All Emerson quotations are paraphrased.

and to accept nothing on secondhand knowledge." He said, "That's what I'd like to do." And he built his career on that idea.

In Emerson's well-known essay "Self-Reliance," he said that "imitation is suicide" and, "Say what is true for you and every heart will respond to that iron string." So Emerson and Thoreau—who also did what was true for him—and Whitman became my guides and have been my guides ever since.

When Emerson was about my present age, he said, "I've been reflecting recently on why I don't have any followers. A lot of other people who have written less than I have, have all kinds of followers." He continued, "I decided the other day that it is because those other people were trying to bring people to them while I've been trying to bring people to themselves." I would want Emerson to know that it worked for me—that his work didn't bring me to Emerson; his work brought me to myself. This is my goal when I work with people and organizations, and I think I picked it up from him all those years ago—to bring people to themselves.

I am so grateful that Emerson's words have allowed me to be who I really am, and I am especially grateful to my wife.

QUESTIONS

✍ *If you were to speak from your own heart and say what is most deeply true for you, what would you be saying these days?*

✍ *And if you were able to build a work life based on those personal truths, what would it be? What kind of work would you be doing? With whom?*

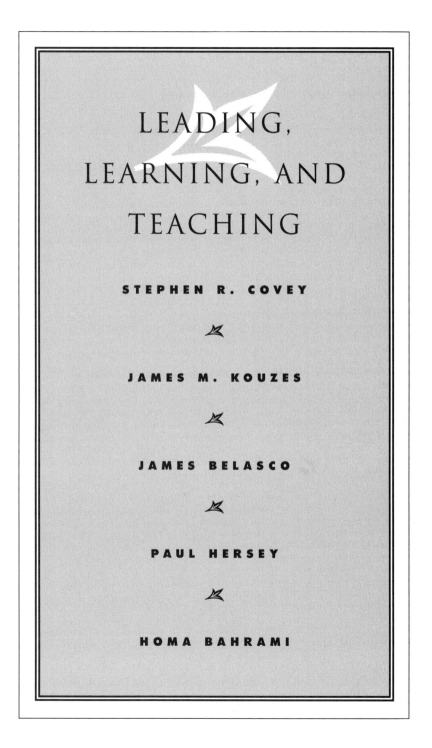

LEADING, LEARNING, AND TEACHING

STEPHEN R. COVEY

JAMES M. KOUZES

JAMES BELASCO

PAUL HERSEY

HOMA BAHRAMI

8

STEPHEN R. COVEY

Stephen Covey is an internationally respected leadership authority, family expert, and teacher. He is an organizational consultant, founder of the former Covey Leadership Center, and vice chairman of Franklin Covey Company. He has made teaching principle-centered living and principle-centered leadership his life's work. Covey is the author of The 7 Habits of Highly Effective People, *chosen by readers of* Chief Executive *magazine as the most influential book of the twentieth century,* Principle-Centered Leadership, *and* Living the 7 Habits, *and co-author of* First Things First. *He has also been featured as one of* Time *magazine's twenty-five most influential Americans. He has received the Thomas More College Medallion for continuing service to humanity, the Toastmasters International Top Speaker Award, and several honorary doctorates.*

Shaping Experiences

I've had many powerfully shaping experiences in my life. In this chapter, I share six of them with you with the hope that my learning journey might be helpful to you.

First, when I was a university student, I had a speech professor who was one of the finest professional speakers in the country.

Copyright © 2000 Franklin Covey Company. Reprinted with permission. All rights reserved. This article first appeared in *Executive Excellence.*

Most weeks, he would travel and give two or more speeches somewhere in the country.

At the end of the semester, I asked him, "If you were to do it all over again, what would you do differently?" He said, "I would institutionalize my work—build an organization, so there could be follow-through on my teaching and speaking."

I didn't know it at the time, but his comment powerfully influenced my decision later in life to supplement my teaching with outside speaking and consulting experiences and eventually to leave my post at the university and start my own company.

Second, while teaching at the university, I met a visiting professor, Dr. Walter Gong from San Jose, California. He taught a class for faculty entitled "How to Improve Your Teaching." It lasted one entire semester. The essence of his program was this great principle: *The best way to get people to learn is to turn them into teachers.* In other words, you learn the material best when you teach it.

I immediately started to apply that principle in my work and at home. When I first started university teaching, my classes only had about 15 to 30 students. When I started applying Dr. Gong's principle, I found that I could effectively teach many more students; in fact, some of my classes were packed with nearly 1,000 students, and yet the students' performance and test scores actually went up. Why? When you teach you simply learn better. Every student becomes a teacher, and every teacher a student.

Now, the common paradigm is that the teacher-student ratio is critical—fewer students means higher-quality teaching. But if you turn your students into teachers, you gain leverage. You move the fulcrum over. Also, when you teach, you implicitly commit socially to live what you teach. In this way learning by teaching beautifully illustrates the second great commandment.

Third, after teaching business executives the importance of having a mission statement and involving members of the organization in its development, I decided to involve my own immediate family in the development of a family mission statement. My mother, my wife, Sandra, and all nine of our children were deeply involved in this activity over a period of eight months. Eventually, we produced this statement: "The mission of our family is to create a nurturing place of faith, order, truth, love, happiness, and relaxation, and to provide opportunity for every person to become responsibly independent and effectively interdependent, in order to serve worthy purposes in society, through understanding and living the gospel of Jesus Christ."

There are four parts to our family mission statement: (1) the characteristics of our home, (2) the effects on the individual, (3) the purpose of contribution, of making a difference, and (4) the source of the power. We put that mission statement up in our home, and we examine ourselves against it every week in a family meeting. How well do we measure up to this? We found that in many ways we fail. But we constantly come back to it, much like a pilot might fly a plane off track 90 percent of the time, making small deviations and course corrections based on feedback from the environment, but eventually arrives at the destination. We found that at any given point in time, we might be off track, but the key to progress was having a clear sense of destination and direction, and continually returning to course. The process of developing a family mission statement inevitably created personal mission statements with us all. I can't begin to describe the immense positive effect that these personal and family statements have had on our family and now on our grandchildren. In our own family, we find that "adopting" other families, particularly those at risk, is one of the best ways to fulfill our mission of trying to make a difference by participating in worthy causes.

Fourth, another extremely powerful shaping experience was my doctoral work, where I reviewed 200 years (1776 to 1976) of the so-called "success" literature of our country. I found that for the first 150 years, the focus was primarily on what I call "the character ethic"—on principles and natural laws that are timeless, universal, and self-evident. Then, over the next 50 years, the focus started to shift toward what I call "the personality ethic"—a focus primarily on image and personality-based influence techniques. And, over the last 25 years, since my doctoral work, there has been an even more pronounced separation from the character ethic. Even though considerable lip service is constantly paid to it, the primary focus of our business and success literature is on appearances, politics, financial gain, and application of new techniques and technologies.

Fifth, the thrust of my background and training has taught me this: *The key to human influence is first to be influenced—first understand, before seeking to be understood.* People are only open to influence when they feel understood. I find in my consulting and training with client organizations that once I understand how people think, what their burning issues are, their deep concerns, I can adapt my approach and gain greater influence, particularly if my approach is based on principles, not just on short-term entertainment or good stories. If I seek first to understand and even have my thinking and my message influenced by their feelings and concerns, I find people are much more open to my influence.

I then try to teach people timeless principles, a new way of thinking—something that can powerfully influence behavior over time—and leave them with a sense of responsibility and a personal commitment to apply these principles in both their personal and professional lives. This way you have a long-lasting impact and influence. When your students or clients get grounded in principles, they cease looking to you for answers. They cease needing external motivation. They become increasingly independent and capable of thinking their own thoughts, coming up with their own solutions and applications, within this new frame of reference. As the Eastern expression goes, "When you give a man a fish, you feed him for a day; when you teach a man to fish, you feed him for a lifetime."

In the Middle Ages, some doctors tried to heal people through bloodletting. The theory was that the bad stuff is in the blood, and so you let it out. If this didn't work, and you didn't question the theory, what would you do? You'd let out more blood, faster. You might get into TQM on bloodletting or you might go into Team Building by putting people in the mountains and letting them do free falls off cliffs. This way, when they return to the bloodletting unit, they will do it with more spirit of cooperation. You might teach them positive thinking techniques, so that they exude positive energy. You might even put the patients into smile training, so that they exude positive energy while you do the bloodletting. But the problem is with the theory, not in the attitude or behavior. When Pasteur and other scientists discovered the germ theory, the fundamental cause of disease, we understood for the first time why pregnant women at the time preferred to be delivered by midwives, rather than doctors, because midwives were cleaner. In war, more people were dying from staph diseases behind the front lines than from bullets. The germ theory explained so much; everything was organized differently. That's the power of a paradigm—a way of thinking, a way of understanding reality.

The power of a paradigm of principles that are changeless, universal, self-evident, and self-validated is that people inwardly know that they are valid and true. For example, one self-evident principle is this: *You can't talk yourself out of problems that you behave yourself into.* If you hope to produce a culture of trust in a dynamic marketplace with world-class expectations and standards, you've got to have trustworthiness. If you hope to have people who are grounded in a set of principles so that they (on their own initiative) network with other people, empathizing and creating new win-win alternatives; if you hope to develop a competence to accommodate the new realities, to cultivate your own immune system, so that no matter what comes, you have the capability to adapt, you need to build into your structures and systems the principles and processes of involvement, accountability, responsibility, and commitment over time.

There is a growing awareness that if we are to solve the massive social problems we face, we need a different mind-set and skill set, based on principles, based on the restoration of the character ethic. You can't fake integrity. It is the integration of your own personality and your relationship with other people.

Sixth, by teaching the *7 Habits and Principle-Centered Leadership* in cultures and nations all over the world, I have learned that these principles truly are universal. If you can get enough people interacting deeply and sincerely as they develop their mission statements, and if you can get them to reflect and listen to their conscience and to ask deep questions, they will come up with the same basic mission statement. They will use different words, but their missions will deal with the four dimensions of life: to live, to love, to learn, and to leave a legacy. "To live" has to do with the physical and economic dimension. "To love" has to do with relationships, with respect and dignity. "To learn" deals with the constant need for growth and development, for bench marking against world-class standards. And "to leave a legacy" is to matter, to make a difference, to contribute.

To make the point about universal principles, I often tell the following story:

On a dark and stormy night, the captain of a ship at sea received a frantic wake-up call.

"Captain, captain, wake up."

"What is it?"

"Sorry to wake you, sir, but we have a real problem."

"What is it?"

"There's a ship in our sea-lane, several miles away, and they refuse to move."

"Tell them to move."

"We have, sir. They just won't move."

"I'll tell them! Move starboard 20 degrees."

The signal returned, "Move starboard yourself, 20 degrees."

"I can't believe this," roared the captain. "Who is this joker? Does he know I'm the captain? Tell him who I am!"

The signal goes out, "This is Captain Horatio Hornblower, the 26th, commanding you to move starboard 20 degrees, at once."

The signal returns, "This is seaman Carl Jones, the 3rd, commanding you to move starboard 20 degrees, at once."

"I can't believe this. What arrogance. We're a battleship. We could blow them out of the water. Let him know who we are!"

"This is the mighty *Missouri,* flagship of the seventh fleet."

The signal returned, "This is the lighthouse."

Though I've paraphrased it a bit, it's a true story, published in the *Naval Proceedings Manual.* They actually interpreted a lighthouse as a ship. Principles are like lighthouses. You do not break them—you only break yourself against them. Foundational principles represent "true north." Because, it doesn't make any difference where you are, the compass will always point to true north, to natural laws and principles. You will also find on the compass another indicator, called the "direction of travel." That stands for your behavior, motive, attitude, direction, and sense of destination If you wanted to go 90 degrees east, you'd put the direction of travel at that mark and follow.

I encourage you to study your "direction of travel" in your personal life and in your organization and check for alignment between your direction and true-north principles. Apply this test to your personal life, your interpersonal relations, your managerial work, your leadership, and your organization. By doing this regularly, you will start to build a culture that aligns itself with principles and with a common vision and mission.

The alignment process is tough duty because many traditions develop in the way the organization recruits, trains, rewards, compensates, and reinforces people. But over time you build the principles of respect and trust and alignment with natural laws throughout the culture.

The real challenge, I find, is to live in alignment with your personal mission statement. For me, it is a constant struggle, even with everything that I teach. I'm grateful for 360-degree feedback in our organization and for feedback from my wife, children, and conscience. I believe God, the Father of us all, is the source of our conscience, and that is why conscience gives us an accurate sense of whether or not our lives are in alignment with those natural laws and principles upon which everything that endures is based.

If you plant a Chinese bamboo tree, you see no growth at all for four years. Finally, a tiny shoot appears. But in the fifth year, this special species of the bamboo tree grows eighty feet! Likewise, people, families, and organizations that build on universal, time-less principles will grow impressively on a strong foundation.

We can make such significant difference in the lives of other people. I know many great teachers and trainers who are doing just that—who are impacting communities, associations, schools, children, students, and families. If we focus on everything in our society but neglect the family, we are simply straightening deck chairs on the *Titanic*. The nature of the work we do as teachers is so significant. T. S. Eliot once said, "We must never cease from exploring. In the end, all of our exploring will be to arrive where we began and to know the place for the first time."

We already know this. This material is basically common sense, but it still is not common practice. We constantly need to upgrade our skills and abilities, and to nurture our desires—and those of others—to live by the character ethic. I echo the words of T. R. Chardin: "We are not human beings having a spiritual experience; we are spiritual beings having a human experience."

All six of these shaping forces have encouraged and empowered me to constantly strive to build for the long term—to build a life, a marriage, a family, and an organization on the foundation of correct principles and the character ethic.

QUESTIONS

⚔ *If you were to live your life all over again, what would you do differently?*

⚔ *What is your mission statement?*

⚔ *If you study your "direction of travel," do you find your personal and professional lives are aligned with your personal mission statement?*

⚔ *Why or why not?*

9

JAMES M. KOUZES

James Kouzes is chairman of Tom Peters Group/Learning Systems and coauthor with Barry Z. Posner of the award-winning books The Leadership Challenge *and* Credibility. *Kouzes and Posner's third collaboration,* Encouraging the Heart, *was published by Jossey-Bass in 1999. Kouzes and Posner are also the developers of the widely acclaimed series of 360-degree assessment instruments* Leadership Practices Inventory. *Cited by the* Wall Street Journal *as one of the most requested executive educators in the United States, Kouzes has conducted leadership programs for such organizations as AT&T, Amgen, Boeing, the Boy Scouts of America, Canon, Charles Schwab, Dell Computer, Honeywell, Johnson & Johnson, Levi Strauss, Motorola, Pacific Bell, Sun Microsystems, and the YMCA.*

Teaching and Training

I needed a job. It was the summer of 1969 and I'd just returned to the United States after spending two years serving in Eskisehir, Turkey, with the Peace Corps. I was twenty-four, still full of the sixties' passion to make a difference, but out of work. I'd taught English as a second language and I'd grown to love learners and learning. Before college I'd toyed with becoming a

Copyright © 2000 James M. Kouzes.

football player, a minister, an architect, or a foreign service officer, but a persistent voice inside kept telling me to teach. By the time I'd completed my Peace Corps service as a teacher of English as a second language, I was certain I belonged in the classroom.

So I headed west to Austin, Texas, where I'd trained for the Peace Corps and had fallen in love with Donna Burns, the woman who became my wife in 1970. My search for a teaching job proved fruitless. While I'd been a secondary teacher for two years, no school system in the United States would accept that experience in lieu of a teaching credential. So I turned my attention to finding a community service job in one of the Johnson administration's war on poverty programs. With the help of my dad—a dedicated career civil servant in Washington, D.C., where I grew up—I got an interview with the Community Program Training Institute. The institute was in need of some young, eager, and inexpensive talent to provide management and interpersonal skills training to employees of the newly founded Community Action Agencies. I got a job with the southwestern region, riding the circuit throughout Texas, Arkansas, Louisiana, Oklahoma, and New Mexico, spreading the gospel and building skills of effective human relations.

I didn't know much about management back then—except for what my dad would tell us over the dinner table—but I had had the opportunity to experience some of the best interpersonal skills training in the world while preparing for the Peace Corps. The National Training Laboratories (NTL), the pioneer of T-groups, played a major role in the Peace Corps' cross-cultural training, and I'd had the benefit of being exposed to their methods beginning in 1969. I was hungry to conduct some of that kind of training myself.

Whatever my new colleagues and I lacked in practical experience, we made up for in energy, enthusiasm, and a strong desire to serve others. Our new employer was also wise enough to understand how important early world-class training was to prepare its new recruits, so they hired the very best to put us through the paces. It wasn't long before I was hooked, and I began the lifelong adventure that has been my career.

In the process of training, I met some of the most seasoned NTL professionals in the business. One of them was Fred Margolis. Fred was a student of Malcolm Knowles, the father of the theory and method of adult learning known as andragogy. Fred was a master, and he taught me a lesson in the early 1970s that has shaped everything I've done as an educator since then.

I was doing some work in Washington, D.C., and after a day of training, Fred and I met at an Italian restaurant for dinner. During our dinner, Fred asked me this question: "Jim, what's the best way to learn something?" Since I'd been extensively involved in experiential learning I confidently told Fred the obvious: "The best way to learn something is to experience it yourself."

"No," Fred responded. "The best way to learn something is to teach it to somebody else!" Wham! Right between the hemispheres! The act of teaching is an act of learning—the deepest kind of learning. You've probably felt the impact of this yourself whenever you've been asked to teach others, whether you're a subject matter expert or a novice.

The moment you're asked to teach you start to think, study, worry, and prepare. In the process you become consumed by learning. You know you're on the line. You're going to have to perform live in front of others and you better know your stuff. You've got to learn at a deeper level. Peter Drucker reveals that this is one of the five leadership lessons he learned from one of his mentors early in his career. "People learn the most," Drucker observed, "when teaching others. My third employer was the youngest of three senior partners of a bank. Once a week or so he would sit down with me and talk about the way he saw the world. In the end, I think he learned more than I did from our little talks."

That lesson—we learn best when we teach someone else—has shaped my style more profoundly than any other lesson on learning. It inspires me daily to find new ways for people to teach each other. Even if I'm asked to give a lecture on one of my recent books, I always try to provide an opportunity for participants to become the teachers. When they put themselves out there as a role model or subject matter expert, as someone who's a credible source of information, I know and they know that they've got to reach inside a lot deeper than if I just ask them to take part in a simulation. I do that, too, but it's the teaching they do afterward that's the most important part of the experience. That's when you know you've internalized it, made it a part of you. And when you've internalized it, you can externalize it; you can teach it to others.

The richness in this lesson has also led me to realize that master teachers and learners are master storytellers. All we know about each other, we know through the pictures we show and the stories we tell. The rest remains hidden. The more effectively I enable participants to reach inside and reveal something they've learned from their own experiences, the more effectively I teach. And the more capable I am at finding and telling my own story, the more authentically I learn. Learning and teaching, teaching and learning—what a joyous adventure it's been and continues to be!

It seems to me there are only two reasons great teachers know more than their students: One, they've dedicated themselves to learning, and two, they love what they're learning. Come to think of it, maybe that's just one reason.

QUESTIONS

⚔ *As a manager or parent, how might you let your employees or children teach you?*

⚔ *How might you become a learning participant, a teacher?*

10 JAMES BELASCO

James Belasco is a professor of management at San Diego State University and the founder and CEO of a global software and service firm. An experienced consultant, he has worked with such companies as AT&T, Royal Dutch Shell, McDonnell Douglas, Frito-Lay, BMW, and Heineken Beer. Belasco is a dynamic speaker on topics of strategy, leadership, change, empowerment, and customer service. He is also the author of nine books, including the best-seller Teaching the Elephant to Dance: Empower-ing Change in Your Organization. *His newest book is* Soaring with the Phoenix: Renewing the Vision, Reviving the Spirit, Recreating the Success of Your Organization.

The Learner's Point of View

One of my most important learning experiences occurred when I was a doctoral student and teaching assistant for Professor Emil Mesics at Cornell University in the School of Industrial and Labor Relations. In his large class, Professor Mesics gave the two one-hour lectures, and his graduate assistants taught the follow-up small group discussion sections.

Each week, the three TAs met with Professor Mesics to put together the topics for the discussion sections, and then each of us went off on our own and taught our particular sections. Professor Mesics observed our classes twice each semester and met with us later to give us feedback on our performance.

Now, Professor Mesics was an unusual professor. He didn't have a Ph.D., having come to his professorship as a practitioner, not a researcher. He pioneered the concept and practice of on-the-job training for the Radio Corporation of America (RCA) during World War II and won many accolades and awards for his efforts. His reputation as a practitioner was precisely the attraction for me. I enrolled to earn my doctorate in 1963, fully intending to return to industry after graduation. The chance to learn from a master practitioner motivated me to lobby hard to become Professor Mesics' TA. I was overjoyed to be chosen and vowed I'd do whatever it took to get a great recommendation from him. I knew that doing well on his observation visits was critical to achieving my goal.

Professor Mesics gave me two weeks' notice of his intention to visit my class. While I appreciated the early notice, it immobilized me. I wanted desperately to be a brilliant lecturer with him in the classroom. Yet I'd never taught before, nor had any formal instruction in teaching methodology. Everything I knew about teaching I'd learned either by watching my dad, who was a high school teacher, or by sitting in a classroom for eighteen years— hardly adequate preparation for excellence. My self-doubts and anxiety about my teaching skill kept me awake for most of the two weeks.

In my usual over-prepare crisis mode, I developed an extensive lesson plan. I coached the class on how to behave on that crucial visitation day. I even promised things that I would not want to repeat here to assure that I'd get the "right" behavior during the critical fifty-minute time period when Emil Mesics sat in my classroom.

On that fateful day, I arrived early at the classroom and wrote my class outline, overhead questions, and key points on the chalkboard. I was pacing the classroom an hour before the first student walked in. The class went better than I ever could have hoped. The students asked good questions. The students answered my questions. The students participated. And my lecture was right on the mark. Afterward Professor Mesics came up to me, shook my hand, and said, "That was a brilliant class. I've taken some notes. Could we talk after the next lecture?" I was on cloud nine when I left the classroom.

After Professor Mesics' next lecture, we went back to his office for our review of his notes, and I was certain I would receive some more praise for the great job I had done. He began, "It was a great class. You are a gifted lecturer. You are energetic and enthusiastic, and that's contagious in your classroom. You engage and involve your students at high levels of discussion. You're a brilliant teacher. Tell me, though, what do you think the students learned?"

His question stopped me cold. I frantically searched for an answer, feeling the sweat begin to break out across my forehead. "Well," I said haltingly, "I had my main points on the board and kept coming back to them. They likely learned them."

Professor Mesics then asked, "How do you know they learned those points?"

I stumbled and stuttered, and finally said, "They answered the questions I put to them. Doesn't that show they learned those points?"

"What is the relationship between the questions you asked and what they really learned? All I heard from their answers was that they knew the answers to your questions, as if the whole exercise had been rehearsed. My question is still the same. What do you think they learned?"

Squirming like a six-year-old boy caught with his hand in the cookie jar, I had to admit, "I don't really know."

Professor Mesics was a kind and gentle man. Sensing my extreme discomfort, he leaned forward and asked softly, "Jim, why do you think I spend fifty minutes with you every week?"

"To learn," I answered meekly.

"Precisely," he said. He then proceeded to dissect my lecture, like a cadaver in the morgue, in terms of my four key points and my questions. At each juncture he asked me what I wanted the students to learn and if I knew whether they had learned it. I couldn't answer a single one of his questions in the affirmative.

Finally he leaned back in his chair and said, "Jim, the most important outcome of that fifty minutes spent in your classroom is not what you do; it's what they leave with. It's not what you teach that's important; it's what they learn that matters most. And the only way you ever know what they learn is to see your lesson plan from their point of view."

Professor Mesics' insight lit my path for a lifetime. I can point to a trillion examples of how seeing it from the learner's perspective made a big difference in my behavior. For example, in every management situation (and all management situations are truly learning situations) I begin by describing the situation from the other players' viewpoints. I then identify how I can best help them be more effective in doing what they need to do.

I've also come to realize the power of another of his messages. Professor Mesics was most proud of his graduates—those people with whom he had worked, who then left to go on to bigger and better things. "Develop successful graduates," Professor Mesics repeatedly told me. They were just words to me when I first heard them thirty-five years ago. Today they are my personal mantra. The graduates of the "Jim Belasco School of Management" are my greatest legacies. For, as Professor Mesics imprinted on my brain, I know that my value as a teacher is measured by the performance of my students. It's not what I do that matters; it's what my students do in life that really counts. I am proud to be one of Emil Mesics' graduates.

QUESTIONS

- *How can you best help your graduates succeed?*

- *What do you want your students to learn?*

- *How will you know if they've learned it?*

11 PAUL HERSEY

*Paul Hersey has been a business professional, an entre-
preneur, a professor of management and organizational
behavior, a department chairman, a dean, and a university president. He is chairman of the board and CEO
of the Center for Leadership Studies, the home of
Situational Leadership®.*

Standing on the Shoulders of Giants

In my freshman year at the University of Arizona, I
decided to major in commercial art. I had always possessed a certain flair for drawing and it seemed like a good choice. I discovered, however, that I had real difficulty doing what other people
wanted me to do and that a career in commercial art would not
suit me. I learned very quickly that ability is not the only factor for
being successful, that you really have to have motivation, commitment, and passion for what you are doing in addition to the skill.

At that point, I changed my career plans and earned a degree in management, a brand new field at that time, at Seton Hall University.

A professor under whom I studied saw something in this eager young student and gave me opportunities to capitalize on my passion and my natural instincts for teaching. He let me cover many of his classes when he was not able to be there, and when he left to work at the Industrial Relations Center at the University of Chicago, he offered me a contract as a research associate. In later years, when I was in a position to counsel students as they developed their freshmen schedules, I would encourage them not to declare a major for the first two years of school. Rather, they should take a broad range of classes from professors who were passionate about the subjects they taught, whether it was social sciences, English, or history. My approach was to help them shift from external motivations such as "My father feels strongly that *this* is the field I should go into" or "Accountants (or lawyers, doctors, and so on) make good money" to the internal ones. A great majority of students would change their majors and go on to do something they wanted to do and not something they were pushed into doing.

When I finished my graduate work at the University of Chicago, I worked full time at the Industrial Relations Center and became a project director. I really wanted to be a college professor but felt very strongly that I did not want to contaminate the minds of young people with just my academic credentials; I wanted to have some practical experience to go with the degrees. While perusing *Fortune* magazine, I read that Kaiser Aluminum was going to build the world's largest aluminum-producing plant in a small town in West Virginia. I got on the phone, offered my services to Kaiser, and was hired as the training director. It was an invaluable experience as I was involved in the startup operations as well as training. I spent three years there and was then ready for a new challenge. I interviewed with several companies that today we would call high tech and spent the next four years with Sandia

Corporation in Albuquerque, where I was responsible for the technical orientation and management training.

I now had ten years of practical experience, and even though it was a financial hardship, I left the industrial world and got a job as an assistant professor at approximately a quarter of my previous salary. I had made that commitment ten years before, and I felt very good about teaching. The opportunity to enrich a student's academic career and even be a catalyst for change was a special one. Even now, more than forty years later, I am continually hearing from students who share with me that I have changed their lives. That's a very powerful impact to have on someone.

While I was at Kaiser Aluminum in the 1950s, a powerful learning event occurred for me. One evening, well after work hours, I was typing some training material when the industrial relations superintendent came in and saw me typing. He hit the ceiling. He said, "The next time I see you at a typewriter, you will get paid as a secretary. We don't pay you to do that kind of stuff." His comment became a turning point for me as I realized that I should be doing the things I do well and be willing to delegate other tasks to those who did them well. Since then I have applied that lesson to ordinary tasks such as mowing the lawn or hiring someone to fix the plumbing. It comes down to capitalizing on one's strengths.

You can take this a step further by helping people find their own greatness. I think everyone has a spark of greatness that needs to be given the opportunity to burn. One of the hardest lessons we all need to learn is to gain confidence in other people and to turn over responsibility—not too soon, mind you, but we can help others get ready to take on that responsibility.

I enjoyed my career in the academic world immensely, but I was reaching only a small segment of the population, even with a full academic load. I decided that I could influence more people by being in the training business and hiring bright, talented young people to work with me. That was how the Center for Leadership

Studies started. Through the center and other Situational Leadership, training programs, I estimate that we reach several million people a year via textbooks, workshops, and videotapes.

If I were to summarize the way I feel about life, I would quote Sir Isaac Newton, who said, "If I have been able to see further than others, it is because I stood on the shoulders of giants." I had the ability to look farther over the horizon by standing on the shoulders of men like Carl Rogers, Douglas McGregor, and Abraham Maslow, giants in the field. I can only hope that I have had an impact on this younger generation of Blanchards, Goldsmiths, and others. Who could ask for better than that?

In Lewis Carroll's *Alice in Wonderland,* Alice arrives at the intersection of many roads; looking up she sees the Cheshire cat smiling from the tree above. She asks the cat, "Which road should I take?" and he responds, "Where is it you'd like to go?" Alice replies, "I really don't know." The cat responds, "Then take any road."

QUESTION

⚔ *Which road should you take?*

12 HOMA BAHRAMI

Homa Bahrami is an internationally known educator, speaker, and author who specializes in knowledge-based enterprises. She is a consultant, designer, and teacher for executive development programs for business and professional organizations worldwide. Bahrami coauthored the textbook Managerial Psychology. *She was a research associate at the Graduate School of Business, Stanford Unversity, and is a senior lecturer and teacher of organizational behavior at the Haas School of Business, University of California, Berkeley.*

Nuturing Learning Partnerships

The source of my life's learning has been a succession of experiences, some of them in my childhood and others in more recent years. These cumulative experiences have evolved into the philosophy on which I base my teaching and my approach to working with clients. There has been no one transformational event, but rather a series of personal interactions over the course of my life that have given me the particular perspective I have as a teacher and a perpetual student.

THREE PLANKS OF EDUCATION

I think of myself as an educator or teacher, whether I am in the role of professor, consultant, mentor, or coach. My philosophy as an educator consists of three planks. The first is empathy. I always try to understand the uniqueness of each individual student and never engage in a standardized "one size fits all" approach. The second plank concerns energy and enthusiasm, or what might be thought of as a sense of passion for the subject I am teaching. Simply put, I do not enjoy teaching things I do not care about. I limit my work to subjects that are important to me and that I can have fun with. The third plank is subject expertise and a willingness to continue to research and learn more about a particular field.

EMPATHY

The importance of empathy, or trying to see things from the other person's point of view, is evident to me largely as a result of my childhood experiences. I am Persian by birth but was raised and educated in England. The experience of growing up in a country and a culture different from the one I was born into affected me greatly. The boarding school I attended brought me in touch with many different cultures, because the students came from all over the world. It was like growing up in a small-scale United Nations.

I learned during my teenage years that one culture measures success differently from another. When I was fifteen, I was invited by a close school friend to spend the summer holiday at her family's home in Kenya. I will never forget the feeling I had as I walked in the door to what, in my mind, was a mansion with a household staff of between twenty and thirty servants. I realized that the number of servants one had was the measure of one's wealth and status in Africa at that time. In England, I observed that success was often measured by where you went to school, your parents' occupations, and what socioeconomic group you belonged to. Having now lived in the United States for many years, I have observed that Americans are measured by what they do and by their tangible accomplishments.

The real insight I gained through my experiences of many different cultures, especially in Kenya, was how different people are and yet how similar we all are. We all want recognition, we all want self-esteem, we all want to better our circumstances, and we all value education in one form or another. Yet those common values are implemented differently from one culture to another. Empathy gives us a way to appreciate that people from different cultures strive to achieve similar things but go about it in quite different ways.

An example of how I apply the principle of empathy in my work is the way I vary lecturing styles. When I teach in Japan or anywhere in Asia, I tend to use a particular style. In Asian cultures, the teacher is the expert from whom students want to absorb knowledge. This is quite different from the approach I find most effective in the United States, which is more facilitating in nature. American students want the opportunity to discuss their own views as opposed to being told what to think. In Europe, I emphasize theory, because there is a high degree of interest in tracing the genesis of a particular idea. I first seek to understand my audience both before and during a particular teaching, counseling, or coaching session so that I am sensitized to what approach will be most effective. My work with people is always anchored in this element of empathy.

ENERGY AND ENTHUSIASM

The words *energy* and *enthusiasm* capture the second plank of my teaching philosophy. Two sets of experiences stand out in my mind as having influenced me to pay attention to these factors. I first developed awareness of their importance as a middle school student in England. The subject of my particular interest was history, which in the hands of many teachers could be very dry indeed. Two history teachers talked about their subjects in a way that was so vivid, so vital and real, it was almost as if I were living the experiences they described.

In one instance, I remember learning about a major battle of World War I, the Somme River battle. My teacher made me feel the pain of the families who suffered and the loss of an entire generation due to the extensive casualties. In this way, history became a living drama in which I felt like a participant instead of a student in a lecture hall. When teachers have energy and enthusiasm for a subject, their passion is what students experience. It is this passion that keeps tough audiences interested and involved week after week.

Energy and enthusiasm were prominent characteristics of two mentors who influenced me greatly when I was a postdoctoral fellow at Stanford in the early 1980s. Hal Leavitt, a very distinguished professor, showed enthusiasm in the form of curiosity. Hal always asked questions and was always interested in the answers. He would probe issues with an almost childlike curiosity that I found engaging. This approach is one that I model in my own work today.

Lee Bach, a very distinguished economist, demonstrated a compelling interest in, and passion for, his subjects. I had the opportunity to work with him as a research associate and witnessed his profound interest in his subjects. He was not satisfied with a single answer to a question and would probe deeper and deeper by asking more questions.

I do not consider myself as much a teacher as a perpetual learner. Whether in front of a classroom or coaching an executive, I did not succeed unless I came away from the session having learned something. I continuously replace the material I use with clients and students and upgrade it with new discoveries, insights, and learning. Hal Leavitt and Lee Bach inspired me to be a teacher who thirsts for knowledge, is never self-satisfied, and is always open to new possibilities.

EXPERTISE

Expertise involves knowing your own limitations and never pretending to be an expert when you do not have sufficient knowledge. This third plank evolved largely out of my work with executives in the Silicon Valley. I observed that in knowledge-based high technology companies, people have a way of seeing through things quickly. A junior software programmer asks her boss a question. The boss has fifteen years of experience and gives a vague and rambling answer. The junior person dismisses the boss as someone who does not have the expertise he purports to have.

Facilitation of executive meetings has also provided me first-hand learning about the importance of subject matter expertise (organization design, for example), as well as knowing when to apply that expertise, when to listen to others, and when to admit I do not know something. When managers of an organization are planning the future of the organization, they dig very deeply into the subject. They require that the outside facilitator be able to add value at the deepest level. Having buzzwords and the latest jargon does not equip a consultant with the in-depth expertise needed to satisfy clients with significant intellectual capital.

The model I follow in working with clients is that I know some things but certainly not everything about my subject. I come to a session with the idea that I will learn from it just as my client will. I know it has been a success if we all come out of the session having jointly created something. I have little regard for the guru approach to learning. I think of my role more as a midwife, helping other people give birth to ideas and to some of my ideas as well. The guru model is irrelevant today and has been replaced by peer-to-peer learning, where teachers and students are collective colleagues in learning partnerships.

Pivotal to the success of this model is the role feedback plays. I have found frequent, interim feedback invaluable in teaching MBA classes. My effectiveness as a teacher will be limited if I can only see things from my point of view. If I solicit feedback periodically, I can make midcourse corrections that help students experience further learning. Seeking feedback is a step that synthesizes the three planks of my philosophy. I need empathy to understand that my students are unique individuals with life experiences solely their own. In asking their opinions, I give them respect and demonstrate that they are valued colleagues in our learning partnership. I demonstrate energy and enthusiasm for the subject by being responsive to their input. Finally, I ask for feedback as a content expert who continually strives to learn more about my subject.

Ultimately, each of us must look deeply into ourselves and answer the hard questions about who we really are, what our priorities are, what we are willing to put up with, and what we simply can't tolerate. The principle to remember is that you can't teach others unless you really know who you are and what makes you tick and until you understand what characteristics will make your teaching and learning most effective.

QUESTIONS

⚔ *What learning styles best suit you? What makes you tick?*

⚔ *What styles have you found that consistently work in teaching others?*

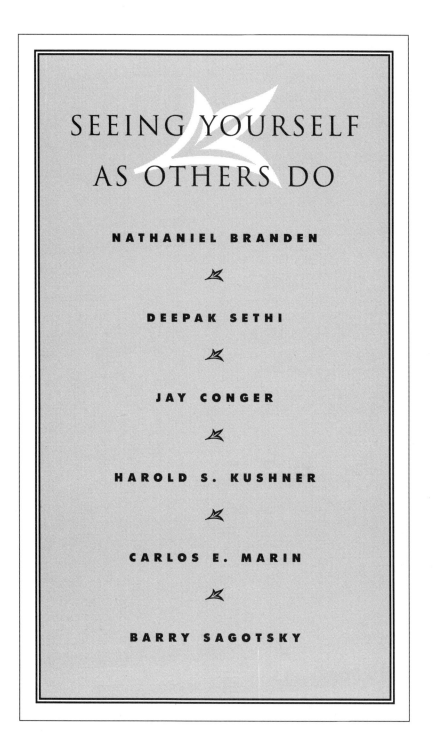

SEEING YOURSELF
AS OTHERS DO

NATHANIEL BRANDEN

DEEPAK SETHI

JAY CONGER

HAROLD S. KUSHNER

CARLOS E. MARIN

BARRY SAGOTSKY

13 NATHANIEL BRANDEN

Nathaniel Branden is a practicing psychotherapist in Los Angeles with a background in philosophy and a Ph.D. in psychology. He does corporate consulting worldwide, conducting seminars, workshops, and conferences on the application of self-esteem principles and technology to the challenges of modern business. Branden is the author of many books, including The Six Pillars of Self-Esteem, Taking Responsibility, *and* The Art of Living Consciously. *His books have been translated into fourteen languages. In addition to his in-person practice, Branden consults via telephone worldwide.*

Reach into Yourself to Understand Others

Anyone who engages in the practice of psychotherapy knows that it is oftentimes as much a learning experience for the therapist as for the client. Nearly thirty years ago, I conducted a therapy group in which there was a man, a few years younger than I, with whom I had great difficulty relating. He was passive to a degree I had rarely encountered; he seemed to have a soul I can only describe as "limp."

He showed up at the group meetings regularly and on time, and he answered questions if asked, but he rarely initiated anything. And for the life of me, I could not make contact with that spark every therapist has to count on—that thing within a person that wants to live, that wants to be happy, that wants to do more than simply lie down and surrender to uncontested pain.

On the infrequent occasions when he would ask to work on his problems, nothing we attempted ever seemed to lead anywhere. If we had what I felt was a productive session, by the following week it was as if it had never happened: He evidently had thought about nothing and retained nothing. I came to think of him as passivity incarnate. I thought of him as "the waif of the universe"—wistful, slack-lipped, helpless, and limp. As the weeks and then months passed, I grew more and more frustrated.

It's always been important to me to give every client I work with the experience of total and absolute respect. But one day with this man, I lost it—I exploded in exasperation and spoke as I had never spoken to a client before or ever would again. I said something like: "I need to tell you what I am experiencing right now. I am feeling that I hate the profession I'm in—hate doing this kind of work. I feel totally incompetent and that our sessions are futile. Nothing I know is worth anything when I'm dealing with you."

Sure, I confined myself to "I" statements and avoided "you" statements, but what I said was devastating just the same. That night, telling my wife about the event, I was horrified by what I had done. It went against everything I believed. It was totally out of character. What was the matter with me?

I could not get the incident out of my mind, and a few days later at dinner with another couple, both of whom were therapists, I described what had happened and my mystified shock at my behavior. The man, Hal Stone, said to me, "May I offer a psychological interpretation?" Of course, I invited him to proceed.

"I don't think," he said, "you have any trouble recognizing and owning most of your emotions: fear, anger, lust, or whatever.

But I suspect there is one feeling you would never permit yourself and therefore would not recognize when it occurred. And yet all of us, simply by virtue of being human, would have to have that feeling once in a while. I'm talking about the feeling of passive helplessness. I suspect that the part of you that would experience such a feeling is disowned, split off from the rest of you, so that you're oblivious to it. And then—in the person of this client—fate sends you a caricature of this disowned piece of yourself. And I suspect that's why you reacted as you did."

Instantly I felt that what he was saying was true.

The next week with the group, I told everyone about what had been revealed to me. I apologized to my client. I said, "If I could not recognize and accept the part of me that sometimes feels as you do, if that part was denied and disowned by me, there is no way I would be able to work with you productively."

My client seemed to come to life in front of my eyes. He felt understood. He felt accepted. After that, therapy took off and we began to make progress. What I learned from this experience was that whatever I deny and disown within myself becomes a limitation on my effectiveness in working with others.

Today, in addition to practicing psychotherapy, I do corporate consulting, and the same principle is operative in that context. If, for example, I am working with a CEO or another executive who is resisting necessary change, I know that if I can make contact with the part of myself that sometimes resists necessary change, I will be more effective. If I am coaching a brilliant engineer who has difficulty working as a member of a team, I know that if I can connect with the part of myself that is attached to being the Lone Ranger, I will be more effective. If I am working with a manager who feels much more comfortable managing technology than managing people, I know that if I can connect with the part of me that can get impatient when people do not instantly grasp what I want them to grasp—and who sometimes hates to be bothered with "psychology"—I will be more effective.

I will be more effective because—being more empathetic—
I will cause the person to feel psychologically visible. Feeling
understood, he or she will be more open to new learnings and
more willing to experiment with new ways of operating.

Self-awareness is the foundation of emotional intelligence and
interpersonal competence.

QUESTIONS

- *Do you know someone who irritates/frustrates/confounds you? What is it about this person that causes you to react as you do?*

- *Can you empathize with this person? Can you see something of yourself in this person, past or present?*

- *Think of some strategies that you use (consciously or unconsciously) to keep from being your "limp" self. Would any of these strategies help this person?*

14 DEEPAK SETHI

*Deepak Sethi, formerly the assistant director of executive
education for AT&T, is director of executive and leadership development for the Thomson Corporation (a $6
billion, 40,000 employee, information publishing
company). He is a leading authority in the field of
executive and leadership development. His work has been
featured in the* Wall Street Journal, USA Today, NY
Newsday, Training Directors' Forum Newsletter,
Corporate University Xchange Newsletter, *and in
the 1998 book* Leadership by Design. *He has also
been quoted in* Business Week, *the* New York Times,
the Washington Post, *the* Miami Herald, *and* The
Economist. *Sethi is the president of New York Human
Resource Planners and is on the board of directors of the
national Human Resource Planning Society. He is also
on the leadership advisory board of the Peter Drucker
Foundation.*

All Change Is Self-Change

I have worked in leadership development for more than a
decade. The primary focus of my effort has been helping managers become more effective leaders. This is the story of the lessons
I have learned in my own development process.

Several years ago, I was working for a large corporation when
a position opened up. This position would have meant a big pro-
motion for me, and I felt I fully deserved it. I had worked hard

toward it for some time, and it was obvious to most everyone that I was the recognized expert and most qualified person to fill the position. But for reasons other than talent and ability, the job went to someone else who was much less qualified. Naturally, I was very disappointed.

Later, I happened to be talking to a consultant friend of mine about my frustration with the outcome. "Life is unfair! It's all about who you know," I complained. My friend listened for a bit and then stopped me midstream. He said, "You know, Dick, what you are saying is absolutely correct. It is often who you know; it's not what you know. Life is not fair. But the question is: What are you going to do about it?"

This innocuous, innocent, tough-love challenge hit me like a ton of bricks. My consultant friend went on to explain that there are always people in this world and at work who will take advantage of you. Organizations are inherently political. But, he explained, there is a big difference between being victimized and feeling like a victim. We have a tendency to complain and blame other people because it is the line of least resistance. You cannot change the world; you cannot change the behavior of your boss, your subordinates, or your loved ones, although we all spend a lot of wasted effort there. You can only work on yourself. "The real challenge," he counseled, "is to accept reality as it is and then to look within and ask, 'What can I do about it?' Please don't let this failure be in vain. Learn from it and move on."

I took time to reflect on this wisdom. I realized that failure can be a blessing in disguise, and it would be a far worse tragedy if I failed to learn from my failure. So I set out on a learning journey, seeking wisdom from a couple of wise people I am blessed to know. Even though I am an avid reader, it has been my deep belief that true learning is a socialization process and that transformative learning happens most effectively in the physical presence of one or more people.

The first person I sought was Marshall Goldsmith, a guru in the field of feedback, who taught me the simple but profound truth that all learning starts with self-awareness. However, the paradox of self-awareness is that one cannot become self-aware through self alone. A major component of self-awareness is seeing ourselves as others see us. To gain this most invaluable gift from others, we need to identify and seek out perceptive people who can help us grow. We must encourage them to provide us with candid feedback. This is not easy. It takes experimentation, which can happen only if we create a relationship of complete trust and a climate of safety.

Having said that, it is extremely important to note that we are all bombarded by what I call "silent feedback" from people at work and at home. There are a multitude of reactions, cues, warnings, previews, body language, signals, whispers, and other forms of unspoken but potent feedback that come our way every single day, which we fail to recognize or blissfully ignore at our own peril. Self-awareness also means being acutely attuned to our environment.

Ron Heifetz, a professor at the Kennedy School of Government at Harvard, taught me the most practical application of self-awareness. He calls it "the ability to be on the dance floor and in the balcony at the same time." This learned ability, to be both in and out of the game simultaneously and to observe ourselves in action, gives us a deep understanding of the real situation and the unique opportunity to make midcourse corrections in real time.

The third person who has been a great teacher to me is Nathaniel Branden, the father of self-esteem. He taught me the connection between self-esteem and self-image and between self-image and success. Self-awareness informs us where we are. Self-image inspires us to a vision of where we want to be. This gap between the two can propel us to action.

Since that fateful discussion with my consultant friend, I have developed a personal gap analysis that I refine on an ongoing basis. I have determined what skills, behaviors, and mind-sets I need to develop, how I am going to develop them, and by when. In this process, I also had to come face-to-face with what I had to unlearn.

Unlearning is often a most difficult precursor to new learning, but as a German philosopher commented, "We should be willing to give up at any time who we are for what we can become."

I have also worked extensively on my self-esteem, by living consciously and proactively and practicing Dr. Branden's six pillars to self-esteem. Self-esteem can be enhanced only by appropriate, consistent, emotionally intelligent behavior. It takes tremendous self-discipline, but there are no shortcuts to self-esteem.

And lastly, I have invested in a personal network. I like to say that my network is much more valuable than my net worth. I know that at the end of the day, no one is self-made. It is always other people who help us learn and help us win in life. Failure is lonely, but success needs company. You cannot win alone.

Now, whenever I face a hurdle, I ask myself, "What are you going to do about it?" I also now know that all change is self-change. It starts from within, and it begins by realizing that we don't know what we don't know.

QUESTIONS

✍ *What are you going to do when things seem hard or unfair?*

✍ *How can you be more aware of silent feedback and act on it?*

15 JAY CONGER

*Jay Conger is a professor of organizational behavior at the
London Business School and senior research scientist at
the University of Southern California. The author of
more than sixty articles and eight books, he researches
leadership, organizational change, boards of directors, and
the training and development of managers and executives.
His most recent books include* Winning 'Em Over:
A New Model for Management in the Age of
Persuasion, The Leader's Change Handbook, *and*
Charismatic Leadership in Organizations. *One of
Conger's greatest passions is teaching. He has received
numerous teaching awards and was selected by* Business
Week *as the best business school professor to teach leader-
ship to executives. As a former archaeologist, he enjoys
living life fully and always with a sense of adventure.*

Lessons on Life from
the Goddess of Love

This is the story of the summer I spent in Aphrodisias, an
ancient Turkish city named for the goddess of love. What I
learned that summer about life, about the passage of time, and
about living life well changed me profoundly.

During that summer, I gained a deep appreciation for the
speck of time each of our lives represents. I learned that the time

we have is precious. The evidence of mortality of the wealthy, powerful, and famous—people whose names are long lost—was a humbling reminder that quests to leave a legacy are almost always a fantasy. My experiences instilled in me a deep belief that we have to find ways to do what is intrinsically rewarding every day of our lives. If we don't, we will waste the experience and lose the precious opportunity of our own short moment here.

I was nineteen that summer and had just finished my sophomore year. An anthropology major, I was lucky to have landed a job with the National Geographic Society. I would be joining a team of archaeologists at Aphrodisias, a remote site in southwestern Turkey, hours away from the nearest city.

This was extremely good fortune, as Aphrodisias was one of the most important cities of ancient times. As a Greek and Roman city, it had enjoyed a span of several hundred years in which it was one of the most important centers for art and architecture. People in every Roman city wanted to have works from Aphrodisias, because its sculpting schools were renowned throughout the region. Unlike most Roman sculptors, who were famous for copying Greek works, Aphrodisians were renowned for their originality.

The city was situated in a valley between two mountain ranges. Its earliest inhabitants were prehistoric peoples who had settled on a very large hill in the center of the valley. Strategically it was a great location because the land was fertile, there was water, and from the hill, approaching enemies could be seen from either direction. Eventually the little town grew into a Greek city and then a Roman city of several hundred thousand people.

My job for the summer was to work with ninety Turkish workmen to unearth the theater of Aphrodisias. The Frenchman who had first discovered it in the 1800s only guessed at the theater when he found fragments of marble seats on the top of that large hill. While prehistoric peoples had built villages there, the Romans saw the hillside as a natural amphitheater and built into it seats rising up the hillside, using the hill as the support system. It had been a huge theater, holding about 4,000 people. But over the millennia, earthquakes and time had filled in the theater, and the upper portions had collapsed and tumbled down into the lower portions. By the Middle Ages, little evidence of it remained. Our job was to unearth the theater, remove the fill, and restore it to its original form.

My crew of workmen came from a village a kilometer away. They walked out to the dig each morning and returned to their village at the end of the day. While the men were friendly, they were a rough-and-tumble crowd who could grow violent over a minor disagreement—the kind of people I had been isolated from as a student. There were other cultural challenges as well. For instance, they spoke only Turkish and, at the outset, I spoke none. Yet I was to be their crew boss. I learned quickly.

Every day our dig took us further back in time. We could see that as the ancient city declined in importance, and ultimately when the Romans left, the grandeur disappeared. The city evolved into a series of small Byzantine villages and then a series of Islamic villages. Parts of these villages were built inside the amphitheater because it was naturally protected. We had to unearth layer after layer of the villages that had risen inside this amphitheater to ultimately expose the original building.

While digging, I'd find coins that had been hidden in the ancient village walls and everyday pottery that had been broken and forgotten. I'd find tools and hordes of seemingly precious possessions that people had hidden away so they wouldn't be stolen. What I began to see most clearly was the passing of time and people. Over the course of the summer, we dug through two thousand years. We were going down almost fifty years each day—the span of a long lifetime in those ancient days. The evidence of lives spent was powerful and moving.

When the workmen returned to their village at the end of each day, our small band of archaeologists had the whole ancient city to ourselves. In the evenings I would always go for a walk in the ruins. There's something magical about the night in Turkey. At dusk, the sky turns a brilliant, rich, pink-orange color, and as the night wears on, the Milky Way extends from horizon to horizon. I was swept away by this breathtaking, natural beauty that highlighted a foreground of ancient temples, marble walkways, and beautiful sculptures. It was as if we had a museum all to ourselves for two and a half months—a museum without a roof, a museum the size of a city that once held 300,000 people.

There was a powerful sense of mystery to the place. The site itself was spectacular, with several beautiful temples, marble streets, storefronts, homes, and palaces. There was an enormous stadium that had held about 20,000 people. I would wander alone at night among these fabulous ruins, and as I walked, the wind would whip through the stadium, and I could hear 20,000 Romans cheer their favorite team.

The poignant realization hit me early on that one day a thousand years from now some young archaeologist would be unearthing my period of time where I had lived. I would be much like the pile of stones and rubble that made up one of the little village houses.

I learned another lesson there, too. The theater, as well as many of the monuments, had been built by very wealthy and powerful individuals whose names were carved on the imposing marble structures. One distinguished person had given this building to the city and another had given that one. At the time, these were the most powerful individuals in the city and, often, powerful citizens of Rome. Yet nobody knows any of them today. They are simply names on a wall. And they had been the most accomplished citizens of their time. The lesson was that no one endures forever. I too shall pass, and whatever fame I might have is brief. Learning this was profoundly humbling.

Shelley wrote of Ozymandias—an Egyptian pharoah whose sculpted head rested in the sand: "My name is Ozymandias, king of kings: Look on my works, ye mighty, and despair!" One sees simply the broken head of the pharaoh; his greatness has vanished.

I began to see firsthand that the impact of powerful people has a limited legacy, despite the fact that they may live on in our public works or art or books. We live on through our children and grandchildren, but that's about it. The lesson is to live well for today, for yourself and for your family. Do not simply hope you will live for what you leave behind.

During this time, I felt a sense of paradox because of the grandeur and mystery of life that was around me. When I wandered through the ancient towns that people once lived and thrived in, I felt connected with a higher power—something indeed eternal. I felt there must be a God out there because I sensed the power of the natural beauty and the human beauty blended together.

Of course, Aphrodite is the goddess of love. And really, what all of this is about—in a strange way—is love. If you love life and you love yourself and you love the people you're with, you have an obligation to develop them and yourself. And if you love yourself, you will always do things for your betterment rather than things that harm you.

Like the Turkish sunsets, that summer at Aphrodisias has colored every day of my life, in that I keenly feel how fleeting and precious time is. It became extremely important for me to discover my gifts and realize my potential early on so I could make my own short time on this planet truly count.

The other lesson powerfully reinforced by the experience of Aphrodisias was the certain knowledge that my name won't really live on—that to spend one's life trying to build a name that will live on is an illusion. Doing what is intrinsically rewarding for me and for the people with whom I live and work is really what is valuable—building a living daily legacy rather than the illusion of a permanent, immortal legacy.

QUESTIONS

- *Knowing that my legacy is not eternal, how shall I live today?*

- *What can you do in your life today that is intrinsically rewarding for you and people with whom you live and work?*

- *How can you be a better teacher and developer of others today?*

16 HAROLD S. KUSHNER

Rabbi Harold Kushner is rabbi laureate of Temple Israel in Natick, Massachusetts, a congregation he has served for twenty-four years. He is best known as the author of the international best-seller When Bad Things Happen to Good People, *which has been translated into twelve languages and named one of the ten most influential books in recent history by Book of the Month Club members. Kushner's latest book,* How Good Do We Have to Be?, *is also a best-seller. Rabbi Kushner has written four other books that have received various honors. A graduate of Columbia University, he was ordained by the Jewish Theological Seminary in 1960 and received his doctoral degree from the seminary in 1972. Kushner has six honorary doctorates.*

Don't Be Perfect

The more I deal with people's problems and the more I look at my own life honestly, the more convinced I am that a lot of misery can be traced to one mistaken notion: we must be perfect for people to love us.

Nothing can make us feel worse than the conviction that we don't deserve to be loved. And nothing will generate that conviction more certainly than the idea that when we do something wrong, we give God and the people closest to us reasons not to love us.

We may get this message of perfection from parents who genuinely love us and who show that love by correcting our every mistake and constantly urging us to do better. We may get this message from teachers who praise only the perfect papers and show impatience when we do something wrong.

Saddest of all, we may have picked up this same message from our religious leaders—that God holds us to strict standards of right and wrong, that He knows every nasty thing we do, even our secret thoughts, and that every sin we commit separates us from God's love. Yet why would God set us up for failure by setting a standard that not one of us could possibly meet?

The best summation of my religious outlook is one I saw on a bumper sticker: "God Loves You Anyway." God may be disappointed in some of the things we do, but he is never disappointed in who we are: fallible people struggling with the implications of knowing good and evil. He knows the difference between the deed that is wrong and the person who is not a lost soul for having done wrong.

We should struggle to be as good as we can, but being human can never mean being perfect. We face situations so complex that no one could get them right all the time. We may even discover that our colleagues like us better when we make mistakes because they see us as more human.

I remember times I had to tell my children I was wrong about something and how fearful I was that they'd lose respect for me. I was astonished to find that they loved me all the more for being willing to admit my mistakes. They needed to be assured of my integrity more than of my perfection.

Sometimes, though, people cannot handle our mistakes. Perhaps our parents need us to be flawless, or our mates harp on our failures because they want us to improve. Perhaps our friends are unforgiving because our failure touched them at a vulnerable time. These responses can make us feel guilty. But before taking on that guilt, we need to ask ourselves whether it's warranted.

Some years ago two elderly women in my congregation died the same week. One afternoon I visited both families. At the first home, the older son said to me, "It's my fault that Mom died. I should have insisted on her going to Florida. I should have gotten her out of this miserable cold weather."

I tried to console him, then made my way to the second home, where the oldest son told me, "I feel it's my fault that Mother died. If only I hadn't insisted on her going to Florida. The abrupt change was too much for her."

If our guilt is appropriate, we should be careful that the emotion attaches to the deed, not to ourselves. The husband who betrays his marriage vows and the wife who abuses the family credit card should feel guilty. Guilt is useful as a motivator to change, but it is useless and destructive when it paralyzes the person with a sense of unworthiness and unlovability.

When we do something wrong, we create a situation in which the good part of our self is at war with our weak, selfish side. We lose the sense of wholeness that enables us to do things that matter most to us.

Life is not a trap set for us by God so that He can condemn us for failing. Life is not a spelling bee, where you're disqualified if you make one mistake. Life is more like a baseball season, where even the best team loses one-third of its games and even the worst team has its day of brilliance. Our goal is to win more games than we lose.

When we accept that imperfection is part of being human, and when we can continue rolling through life and appreciating it, we will have achieved a wholeness that others can aspire to. That, I believe, is what God asks of us, not "Be perfect," not "Don't ever make a mistake," but "Be whole."

At the end, if we are brave enough to love, strong enough to forgive, generous enough to rejoice in another's happiness, and wise enough to know there is enough love for us all, then we can achieve a fulfillment that no other living creature will ever know. We can enter paradise.

QUESTIONS

- *Can you accept your imperfections?*

- *Are you willing to admit mistakes to your children or students?*

- *How can you best teach this important lesson about imperfection to your students?*

17 CARLOS E. MARIN

Carlos Marin is a partner with Keilty, Goldsmith &
Company. He is the former vice president of the Human
Development Training Institute in San Diego and the
former academic dean and chancellor of National
University. Marin is also one of the founders of the
National University campus in San Jose, Costa Rica.
An experienced international consultant and leadership
development educator, Marin has worked with such
companies as American Express Companies, Bell South
Telephone Company, the Coca-Cola Company, Kodak,
and Texas Instruments. He has been a lifelong student
and practitioner of several martial arts, specifically t'ai
chi ch'uan, tae kwon do, aikido, and karate do (shito
ryu style).

Before Lunging Forward, Take a Step Back

Try to recall a time when something just came together in your mind, when you had a wonderful "aha!" experience, when you "got it." Recall that effortless, powerful feeling that comes out of experiencing harmony between the intellectual, the emotional, and the physical parts of us.

I have spent much of my life practicing martial arts and experiencing important learning breakthroughs from the teachings of these disciplines. As a young teacher of high school students, I became curious about the fact that some students would often credit me with the ability to make things easy for them to understand. Later in my career, people would come to me after I had taught a class or facilitated a group and express how I had helped them "connect" with the content of the presentation. Often they would relate how they had "experienced" the material. As I reflected on what I was doing, I related my teaching to my experiences in martial arts.

I came into martial arts with the desire to learn about self-defense. As a kid, I had several episodes and encounters in which my ability to take care of myself was questionable. I was twelve years old when, encouraged by my father, I went to watch a judo class. I found the experience so interesting that I asked my folks to let me sign up for lessons. I was fortunate to start with a teacher (sensei) who was patient and demanding at the same time. Over time, he encouraged me to develop the discipline to train consistently and to experience going beyond the self-imposed limits of what I thought I could do. The more I practiced, the more confident I became, learning to be more quiet inside and more aware of my surroundings.

This process began to influence the way I approached my social world. In judo class we worked on "sensing" the movement and breathing of others. I would ask for explanations of how to do this, and Sensei's response was, "Let your body do it. Don't think—just do it." How could I learn something I did not understand? "Practice, practice," he insisted; and practice I would. This training in perception was helping me develop the ability to focus, to "tune in," and to sense signals from people.

My formal educational process emphasized the importance of rationality, analysis, and conceptual understanding. I was taught to approach challenges with an analytical mind-set, to separate the parts of a problem in order to come to a solution.

As I continued my learning journey in the martial arts disciplines, I was fortunate to meet Al Chung Liang Huang, a gifted tai chi teacher, who once said to me, "Soften your eyes and you will see more." I was in the "trying hard to see" mode, attempting to make sense of a section of the tai chi form we were doing. As I practiced his suggestion, I became aware of the tension in my eyes; I began feeling the muscles of my eyes relaxing and my visual field expanding. This process is equivalent to changing lenses, where patterns of connections and dynamic interrelationships are highlighted.

In the practice of a tai chi form called "the five elements," the first movement is a deliberate step backward accompanied by an opening gesture of the arms. This is not just a physical gesture; it is a psychological one. It is a "clearing" movement aimed at emptying one's perspective to allow the surrounding realities to fill your senses. The message is simple: before you lunge forward, take a step back, as a wider field may present you with more options.

In my work, I often see people craning their heads forward, frowning, squinting their eyes, struggling to understand, to analyze, and to unearth the logic in what they perceive to be happening. When they walk, it seems as if their heads are moving ahead of the rest of their bodies. I see and feel their frustration, their tension. I can hear the stress in their voices, and I invite them to take a deep breath, to sit back and relax for a moment, and to sense what is happening as opposed to thinking about it. I may also suggest that they sense their problem from this new place—a place that requires a softer, but by no means weaker, attitude.

Helping people make a transition to a more relaxed, attentive state enables them to see in renewed ways. Over the years, I have played with this process, and it has become an important tool in my professional practice. It helps people learn more about themselves and others.

First, clear your inner space by suspending your assumptions. Take a step back, and soften your eyes. Now see with new eyes that can take you on a learning journey of your own, where you are a more refined instrument of perception. With practice, your renewed and softer eyes may help you find the experience that leads you to that "aha" feeling or that harmonious "I got it" sensation.

QUESTIONS

⚔ *Can you let your expert eyes relax so that you may see what your expertise may be covering up?*

⚔ *Is stress or tension stopping you from seeing solutions?*

⚔ *How can you apply this tai chi move to help yourself and others see with new eyes?*

18 BARRY SAGOTSKY

*Barry Sagotsky is vice president of the Pacesetter Group
in Princeton, New Jersey. He consults in business
strategy, management strategy, and team and organization development. Before joining Pacesetter, Sagotsky
managed training and consulted internally for Schering
Plough Pharmaceuticals. Prior to that he was at Janssen
Pharmaceutica, a division of Johnson & Johnson. He
founded Sagotsky Multimedia, a training media distri-
bution company.*

It's Not Personal

For me, learning has been a constant activity. As long as
I can remember, I have been interested in many topics, often to the
point of overload on my schedule. Rather than compromise and
possibly miss an experience, I always wanted to try something
new. For most of my life, this constant striving was to prove who
I was to others, to be valued, to be worthwhile. But over time I've
come to realize that you are not valued for what you do nearly as
much as for who you are.

This came home to me for the first time about ten years ago at a meeting of structural thinking professionals I attended in the Caribbean. Robert Fritz, my dear friend and teacher of fourteen years, led the workshop.

One day during the workshop, Robert gave us the assignment to "do what you want to do this afternoon." This sounded easy enough. I decided that I would try scuba diving again. I was somewhat wary due to the simple fact that when scuba diving, your life is dependent on air. You are under water, and there is no air except what you have in the tank on your back. Pushing my worries aside, I decided to dive. But then when I found myself out in a little boat, going through the preparations to dive, my fear began to solidify. I changed my mind and decided not to go into the water.

The next day, back in the conference, I happily reported that I had done what I wanted to do: I had not gone in the water. Robert replied, "No, you didn't. You didn't want to go diving. You didn't do what you wanted to do. If you had wanted to do it, you would have figured out some way to dive." He then asked me why I thought I wanted to dive anyway. My interests at the time included martial arts, motorcycles, skiing, photography, and motorsports/racing. I said, "The truth is, I've always had this fantasy about being James Bond." Robert replied, "Well, I've got the cure for you. Repeat after me: My name is Bond, James Bond." I did this in the presence of the entire group. This succeeded in releasing the tension of the moment, and I felt a mixture of embarrassment and relief.

The next day one of our assignments was to introduce ourselves in two minutes. I was in the back of the room, and as I waited for my turn, I struggled with how I could do this seemingly simple task, given my experience of the previous day. Eventually it was my turn. I went to the front of the room and began to introduce myself. From the back of the room, Robert boomed out, "Do James Bond!" So I did. "The name is Sagotsky, Barry Sagotsky." With appropriate accent and physical presentation, I proceeded to introduce myself through this persona. It was a very emotional experience.

The personal learning in this seemingly simple experience was incredible and has lasted to this day. It was a catalyst for tremendous learning about who I really am, how people see me, and how I see myself. Most important, I learned about my relationships with other people. This learning has proven useful while consulting, facilitating, performing magic, sparring, and learning karate—and every other aspect of my life that involves other people.

I used to focus on doing things and talking about things to impress people, to have them like me for what I did or how I did it, and not for who I am. But now I realize it isn't what I do but who I am that is important to people. Instead of trying to manipulate people into seeing me in a particular way, I am more forthright, saying, "This is who I am." They are free to accept me or not, like me or not. That event was the first time I was aware of the performance I put on to try to impress people.

Now I join with the groups I am involved with. I ask them what they want to walk away with. I support them in that quest and learning. I tell them the truth as I see and know it. I am not upset if they don't get it or if they don't want to get it. At the same time, I'm separate from the group and can leave them free to learn or not, participate or not. It's not personal. It's about the relationship, and that makes it very easy to support others' learning.

QUESTIONS

- *Are you willing to take chances and make mistakes in favor of your learning?*

- *What sorts of things are you afraid of? Are they really things to be feared?*

- *Do you really have any control over the people in your life? In your classes? Your clients? Are they really free to learn or not, practice or not, experiment or not?*

DEVELOPING
SELF-KNOWLEDGE

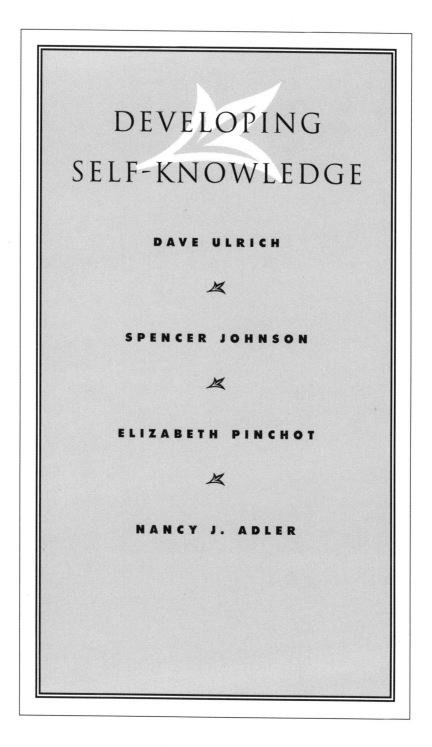

DAVE ULRICH

SPENCER JOHNSON

ELIZABETH PINCHOT

NANCY J. ADLER

19 DAVE ULRICH

Dave Ulrich, a professor at the School of Business at the University of Michigan, was named by Business Week *as one of the world's top ten educators in management and the top educator in human resources. He is the author of eight books, including* Human Resource Champions: The Next Agenda for Adding Value and Delivering Results *and* Results-Based Leadership. *Ulrich has served on the editorial boards of four publications and was editor of* Human Resource Management Journal *from 1990 to 1999. His current research involves results-based leadership, human resources, speed, learning, and culture change.*

An Allegory for Learning

I was twenty-five years old and had been married four years. We had a young child and another on the way. We had just moved to Los Angeles, where I had started a doctorate program and was trying to eke out a living. And I decided to do something bizarre. In a casual conversation with my father, who was nearing fifty, I asked if he ever got bored (he did) and if he ever wanted to do something out of the ordinary (he did).

In mid-March, in an offhand way, I suggested we ride our bikes from Seattle to Los Angeles in mid-June. On the map it looked downhill. Both of us were casual cyclists at best and could be described by those being gracious as "heavy" or "robust." My bike cost $99 and had a name sticker taped over the original manufacturer's name. My dad's bike was not much better. Neither of us had been on much more than weekend rides, but, after getting approval from our spouses (with more faith than confidence), we trained for three months and set off on the adventure.

It was a wild ride to say the least. We carried all our gear and food. We did not have great maps to highlight the biker-friendly roads, but we started at the crack of dawn every morning and rode until we were too tired to ride anymore. We did not use fancy biking gear. We experienced bike riding on dirt roads when we got lost; sleeping on picnic tables when we could not find a city nearby and in church basements when we found a city; almost being run off the road by logging trucks when we were on roads with no shoulders; and the joys of broken brakes, flat tires, and replaced spokes. We also received countless honks, signs, and gestures from motorists. But we made it all the way to Santa Monica. After twenty-one days, we completed the 1,400-mile journey.

This experience became an allegory for many challenges I have faced and lessons I have learned in my last twenty years as professor, researcher, and consultant.

First, I learned about the challenge of balance. My father and I decided to take off in the middle of my doctorate program and while I was struggling to make money. It was difficult for me to be away from my family for twenty-one days. To ease some of the pressure, my wife and child met us partway, and the ride became a family trip. But it wasn't time off from my doctorate. Even while spending time with family and bike riding, I lugged Marvin Dunnette's large and heavy *Handbook of Industrial and Organizational Psychology* with me, and by the end of the trip I had worked my way through all the chapters.

Balance of work, family, and personal life has continued to be one of the major challenges of my life. I constantly recalibrate how I am doing in meeting the multiple demands I place on myself. This trip helped me form a pattern of facing this issue head-on, and of being willing to take time for personal and family matters as well as work. I still try to schedule getaways with family and friends, times when work takes a backseat to simply being together.

Second, I learned to take risks. This entire venture was risky. We did not train well. We did not have the proper equipment. We did not map out the journey. We merely said we would do it, fixed a date, met in Seattle, then started to ride south. In retrospect, we could (and probably should) have planned and prepared more thoroughly. But this way I learned to expand my threshold for risk taking.

Understanding my risk threshold has been enormously helpful in my career. I frequently find myself in meetings with senior managers from large, complex firms who are struggling with very difficult issues. After they share their challenges, they often look to me for ideas. At times I wonder, "What in the world am I doing here? I don't have a clue how to deal with this problem." Then I take the risk, become engaged, and muddle through, generally finding that by asking questions, communicating openly to spark dialogue, and continually reframing, I turn risk into results. It was on the bike trip that I learned to face risk and move forward. This has served me well.

Third, I learned about myself. I discovered that I like to achieve. It felt good to clock the miles, to set daily goals and meet them, and to accomplish the overall task. I found that while I generally like to collaborate, at times I am competitive. On the last Sunday of our trip, we were in Oxnard, California. By this point, while I was still heavy and my old bike was loaded with gear, I was in peak bike-riding condition. As we rode through Oxnard, another biker, on an expensive bike with narrow tires and dressed in biker's attire, pulled alongside my dad and me. He looked the part as he went by us. I grinned at my dad and said, "Watch me." I caught him on the flat land, then blew by him on the long hill. I could hear him struggle to catch me, then give up as I crested the hill. I had not had then (nor have I had since) many athletic accomplishments in my life, and this felt great.

My achievement and competitive drives have both served and hurt me. I push myself hard to achieve, which helps me to raise my self-expectations and do more than I might have otherwise done. But at the same time, I've had to learn to temper my tendency to compete by beating others rather than by extending myself. Understanding, then allaying, my competitive tendency has helped me collaborate rather than vie.

Fourth, I learned about failure. Numerous times on the trip, I felt ready to quit. When my spokes started to snap, when I had the third flat tire, when a logging truck nearly ran me off the road, when my rear end hurt so much I could hardly stand it, I nearly stopped the abuse and said "Enough." But we kept going, and my tolerance for failure and discouragement grew.

This tolerance for failure has served me well. I could cover my walls with rejection letters for manuscripts I felt were more thoughtful and well researched than reviewers did. I have had numerous clients who weren't affected by my ideas the way I thought they would be. I have learned that when things go wrong, I simply need to go forward, learning from the past, but not being bound by it. It still hurts to fail, but moving forward is a useful response.

Finally, I learned about what matters most. By biking together with my father, I came to appreciate him in marvelous ways. For twenty-one days he was my constant companion. We talked to each other, helped each other, shared experiences, and built a bond that endures to this day. I try to share similar experiences with my daughters and son, and I hope that if one of them calls me in eight years to do something bizarre, I will stop my work and go.

In my work, I have found that relationships matter more than projects. I find myself seeking and nurturing relationships of trust with clients. I find many professional colleagues have become friends. It is a joy and a delight to share both personal and professional experiences with my clients and colleagues.

Since the bike trip, I have been on others with young men from my church. We have ridden from Ann Arbor to Mackinaw Island, to Kentucky, and to Niagara Falls. Each trip (from 300 to 500 miles) has taught me new lessons, but none matches the original venture in meaningful silliness, in risk taking with resolve, and in building relationships over time.

QUESTIONS

⚒ *How often do we do things that are out of the ordinary?*

⚒ *How well do we learn from these extraordinary experiences?*

⚒ *How well do we find learning in multiple settings?*

20   SPENCER JOHNSON

Spencer Johnson, M.D., is an internationally respected thought leader, speaker, and author whose insights have helped millions of people discover simple truths they can use to have healthier lives with more success and less stress. He is author and coauthor of the #1 best-selling books Who Moved My Cheese? *and* The One-Minute Manager® *(with Kenneth Blanchard). Other best-sellers include* The Precious Present, Yes or No, ValueTales®, *and five books in the* One Minute® *series:* The One Minute Sales Person, The One Minute Mother, The One Minute Father, The One Minute Teacher, *and* The One Minute for Yourself. *Johnson's books have been featured on CNN, the* Today Show, *and the* Larry King Show, *and in* Time Magazine, Business Week, *the* New York Times, *the* Wall Street Journal, USA Today, *Associated Press, and United Press International.*

Integrity or out of Tegrity?

My learning journey began in deep pain, but the lessons I learned led me to a wonderful place, a place I gratefully enjoy today. There was a time, about twenty years ago, when, after I had enjoyed some success, things began to go wrong. It was like the confluence of a river—everything bad came at once (for which I am now grateful; the pain was sufficient to force me to go through it).

Several projects were faltering and I was under financial stress. My life was out of balance. I was going through a divorce. At one level my life had been working, but at much deeper and more important levels it was not working at all. The worst part of it was that it came as a surprise to me. I thought that everything was all right. I thought I was as honest as most people are, but I had been kidding myself.

I went off by myself to take a long, hard look at the life I'd been living. I went to an isolated area where there was no television or radio to distract me. I spent a lot of time walking empty beaches, sort of blank-minded. I just didn't know what had gone wrong with my life. I began to look at when my life had worked and when it hadn't. I spent time alone, day after day, walking or sitting and staring at the water, reflecting on what had happened.

I knew that I wanted to change, but I didn't know what was wrong or how to change. I certainly had a desire to stop the pain, although the pain was becoming a great teacher. It helped me decide that I couldn't continue to live the way I had been living.

I took a panoramic look at my life and saw it as a series of events. After a lot of time being quiet, being still, I began to see some patterns emerge. When I looked back on the areas of my life that worked, I noticed a certain pattern, and when I looked at the areas that didn't work, I saw the opposite pattern. By looking at what worked and what didn't work, I came to the realization that when I was aware of the truth and I lived it, my life went very well. But when I either didn't see the truth or wanted to ignore the truth and proceeded in spite of it, my life didn't work very well. Eventually there were painful consequences. Once I saw the cause of my pain, I began the journey of learning my lesson.

I became intrigued with the challenge of looking for and living the truth—particularly the obvious truth that I wasn't able to see. When I saw it, it became embarrassingly simple. How could I have missed it for so many years? Looking for the truth became my cornerstone. What I learned was that I had the ability to kid myself, to tell myself something that I believed was true but that was never true. My challenge was to start telling myself the truth as often as I could.

I use the word *integrity* to mean telling myself the truth, and the word *honesty* to mean telling others the truth. Once you have integrity, it's fairly easy to have honesty. For me the challenging part was to develop a sense of integrity—which is what you do when no one is watching. I had found out the hard way that getting "out of tegrity"—a state where you lie to yourself, are unaware of it, and believe what you tell yourself—leads to some very serious pain.

Once we go "out of tegrity" we don't see the problems that are coming, problems that we have created. If we can convince ourselves of something that isn't true, we can be pretty persuasive in convincing others, and if we go down a road at the end of which is a lie, everyone involved will experience pain sooner or later. When I look around the world, it seems to me that the source of all pain is a lack of the truth. So, considering the fact that I don't want to spend a lot more time in pain, whether it's financial, physical, or emotional pain, it's important to me to stay "in tegrity," to do all I can to see reality and tell myself the real truth.

Something else I eventually learned from my experience—when the pain subsided—is not to be too hard on myself, to lighten up and have some fun, to enjoy myself even when I realize I have been wrong and have a lot to learn. Now I ask myself, "Have I kept a sense of humor?" I have found that the balance between truth and humor is very nurturing, and ironically, it's very productive. The interesting thing about humor is that humor isn't concerned with productivity. It's just interested in enjoying the moment.

Of the books I have written, my favorite one is *The Precious Present,* because it is about enjoying the moment. That book practically wrote itself very shortly after the time I was on that remote island. I wrote the first half of it in a couple of hours on cocktail napkins while returning on a boat from Catalina. And I wrote the second half a week later one day on my patio. Because it took only two days to write, I was clear that, in a sense, I didn't write the book. It just came through me, effortlessly. I knew I was getting in touch with the truth, because there was not much ego and more ease.

I have learned that when we are in harmony with reality, things happen very easily. It really doesn't take much effort. It's when we're out of tegrity that we have to stop and say, "Wait a minute. Something's wrong here; I'm working too hard at this."

I have come to ask myself, "Can you feel yourself *feel?*" Up until those long days spent walking the beaches, I had done too many things in my life based on thinking rather than feeling. I had read; I had analyzed; I had thought. I was intellectually educated (Harvard, the Mayo Clinic, and the Royal College of Surgeons) to respect the complicated and discard the simple. I came to realize that what is true for me is pretty much the opposite of what I was taught. I discovered that the simple is much more powerful. Not the simplistic—simplistic is less than what we need. But the simple is all we need and nothing more. And I have never found a great practical truth in my life that wasn't so simple that it was almost embarrassing when I finally saw it.

Another lesson I learned from my painful experience is that our emotions and our egos and our beliefs are not very important. When we laugh we tend to confirm this. Once we get all of that out of the way, we can have a lot of fun being very productive, because the process is not centered on us; we've gotten out of the way. This is a good way to live and a lot more enjoyable for ourselves and for the people around us.

In former days I tried to make things happen. When I realized I needed to let go, to trust in reality and let things happen, everything improved.

The result of living in tegrity for me is that life has gotten dramatically better. I am now joyfully remarried to a wonderful woman, one with great integrity. I have two young sons and our family has a wonderful life. So for me this issue of being in tegrity is very, very practical.

I must acknowledge, of course, that I still fall out of tegrity. There are times when I am not aware and not clear. I still make dumb mistakes, but I hope they are fewer each year. I am more and more aware of the need to stay in touch with reality, to tell myself and others the truth—and enjoy it!

QUESTIONS

- *Am I telling myself the truth, or am I kidding myself?*
- *Integrity or out of tegrity? Which is more enjoyable?*

21 ELIZABETH PINCHOT

Elizabeth Pinchot is an executive coach, consultant, and author, with thirty years of experience to bring to her clients. For the last decade, as cofounder and president of Pinchot & Company, she has coached and trained senior executives in many large organizations as diverse as the U.S. Forest Service, the Canadian National Railroad, and the New York Stock Exchange. Prior to Pinchot & Company, Pinchot cofounded and ran several businesses, including a manufacturing business and a teacher training center, and was a founding staff member of the first computer-assisted education project—a joint venture of IBM and Stanford University. Pinchot is coauthor, with her husband, Gifford Pinchot, of The Intelligent Organization.

Sometimes It Takes an Elbow in the Ribs

She sat down next to me in the front row of an auditorium where E. F. Schumacher was about to speak, and in minutes she had fallen asleep. Margaret, a small, round woman in this last year of her life, was dressed in a navy blue cloak that covered her body, so that as she slept in the chair only the short gray hair on top of her head suggested a human.

I knew I was sitting next to Margaret Mead, who had cofounded the discussion group I was attending in Westchester in the mid-1970s, but I had never met her. I had only had her pointed out to me from the other side of the room. Her close presence excited me at first, but after a while my attention was fixed on Schumacher, who was speaking strong words with a demeanor of gentle and humorous wisdom. He was making sense, and he was very appealing.

During the question-and-answer period with Schumacher, Margaret continued to sleep, but I began to get agitated by the stupidity of a debunking question asked by an elegant woman in Gucci jeans and high-heeled boots. She was saying that ecological agriculture was unworkable and laughably naïve. She was acting like an authority, like the harsh voice of reason. I wanted to speak up to her but didn't dare. You have to picture me—I was in my fifth year of residence on an ecological agriculture commune and looked the part, with long hair, clothes from India, not Italy, and muscles. I felt out of place with this crowd of real grown-ups in the Tarrytown Conference Center, housed in the Mary Biddle Duke Estate overlooking the Hudson River. I couldn't talk in front of strangers.

As Margaret slept on, the woman argued on with Schumacher, and I must have finally gotten angry enough to mutter something hostile under my breath. From the dark-cloaked lump sleeping next to me an elbow shot out into my ribs, hitting hard, and Margaret Mead hissed in my ear:

"Stand up and make yourself heard."

I did, as best I could. I couldn't have done otherwise. I like to remember that elbow in my ribs. I still need it.

QUESTIONS

> *How can you make yourself heard?*

> *What steps can you take to present your ideas more confidently?*

22 NANCY J. ADLER

Nancy Adler, Ph.D., is professor of international management at the Faculty of Management, McGill University, in Montreal, Quebec. She conducts research and consults on global strategy, leadership, and cross-cultural management. Adler is the author of numerous articles and three books, as well as the producer of the film A Portable Life. *She has consulted for private corporations and government organizations on projects in Asia, Europe, North and South America, and the Middle East. Adler has received numerous awards, including Canada's top university teaching award, ASTD's international leadership award, and Sage's management research award. She can be reached at (514) 398-4031 or via e-mail at Adler@management.Mcgill.ca.*

Recognizing Leadership, Trusting Life

Call it serendipity, destiny, or anything else you choose, but a wonderful learning experience happened because a colleague walked into my office one afternoon with a newspaper article that turned out to have an enormous impact on me.

The story is this: I was invited to give the keynote address at the Salzburg Seminar's worldwide conference on global leadership. This conference was of particular interest to me because, for the first time in the fifty-year history of the Salzburg Seminar, the focus was to be on global women leaders. Anyone who knows me even vaguely knows I am very interested in global leadership and in women leaders from around the world. Initially, however, due to other commitments, I didn't give the conference organizers a definite yes, because I wasn't sure I would have enough time to prepare the speech on women leaders that I would really want to give.

Not long after I received the invitation, I was working in my Montreal office when a colleague walked in and said, "Nancy, my mom, who is a business reporter for the *Chicago Tribune,* just sent me this article about Charity Ngilu, the first woman ever to run for president of Kenya. She thought you'd be interested in it." As I began reading the story, I was amazed. If I had combined all my research on the forty-seven women who have served as president or prime minister of their respective countries and had tried to write a definitive case study on women leaders, highlighting the courage and drive it takes to become a country's number-one leader, I couldn't have invented a story more compelling than Charity's.

As another colleague said later, it was *b'shert,* or destined. My own upbringing, however, had taught me not to trust in such coincidences. Why? The reason is simple. My mother came from Vienna and left Europe after Hitler marched in. Her family maintained the attitude that you make the important things happen in your life that are positive; they don't just happen to you.

For me, the very concept of synchronicity—of good things happening by coincidence—hadn't even occurred to me until the previous summer, and then only because of the persistent prodding of an artist friend of mine. She had challenged me to notice three positive things that happened to me each day for a week. The good news is that after a few days I began noticing the positive coincidences that were constantly arriving in my life. The bad news is that it had still never occurred to me that positive coincidences—or synchronicity—had anything to do with my professional life.

By the time I finished reading the *Chicage Tribune* article, the speech I wanted to write flowed from my fingertips onto the paper. The process was nothing like my typical style of writing and rewriting my carefully crafted and well-researched speeches. Rather, the speech just arrived on the paper. It was Charity Ngilu's story, but in my voice, surrounded by the voices of all the other women who have succeeded in leading their countries. Only after the speech had arrived on my paper did I spend a few days checking the facts behind Charity's story. After all, once a professor, always a professor.

I flew to Austria for the opening of the Salzburg Seminar. That evening, when I walked to the podium to deliver my keynote address, the words flowed from my mouth, much like they had flowed from my fingertips onto my paper a few weeks earlier as I wrote the speech.* Even though I give many speeches, I normally get slightly nervous when I deliver a major address to a large international audience, but not this time. I was strangely calm. I didn't even look at my notes.

As I finished the speech, a wonderful Ghanaian woman, a member of Parliament, stood up and told the audience that Charity was her friend and that my speech was very important. Suddenly, Charity became even more alive for me; it was as if she were there in the room.

The next morning, a member of Uganda's Parliament (who had not been able to attend the opening session of the conference the evening before) introduced herself, apologized for having missed my speech, and told me that she had spent the previous evening eating dinner with Charity Ngilu. She carefully explained to me that that the only thing the world community can do to help leaders like Charity is give them global visibility. Global visibility is important because it makes it much more difficult for anyone to silence or harm people such as Charity who are trying to make a

---

*Adler's Salzburg Seminar keynote address is published as "Did You Hear? Global Leadership in Charity's World." *Journal of Management Inquiry,* 1998, 7(2), pp. 135–143.

difference in the world. As the Ugandan member of Parliament explained, global visibility would help Charity maintain her courage. She repeated what the Ghanaian woman had said the evening before: "Nancy, your speech is very important. Your speech gives Charity visibility, global visibility." Visibility reduces the possibility that courage will be extinguished.

The entire experience had somehow become larger than life. Although people often compliment me on being a good speaker, this time it was as if I had become a conduit through which Charity's story and, what is more important, its meaning, had been delivered. Yes, I had recognized the story and its importance, but I had not created the story—I had merely retold it.

The story isn't about me, it's about Charity Ngilu. But it really isn't about Charity, either. It is about having the courage to make a difference in the world; it is about having the courage to speak out.

Trusting my instincts and letting my intuitive side run the show, allowing myself to become a conduit for the story rather than its scholarly creator, was new to me. I have confidence in my academic and consulting experience. I have studied, learned, taught, and contributed to students, managers, executives, and organizations, but this other way of creating and contributing, this intuitive level, is something special. Serendipitous? Synchronous? I am not saying that I completely understand it, but I am now much more open to its possibilities.

QUESTIONS

⚔ *How do we recognize wisdom that is bigger than our personal experience?*

⚔ *How do we trust intuition before we have proof?*

⚔ *How do we address the world community rather than limiting ourselves to any of our more circumscribed local audiences?*

⚔ *How do we let life bring out the very best in us?*

UNLEARNING
WHAT YOU
THOUGHT
WAS SO

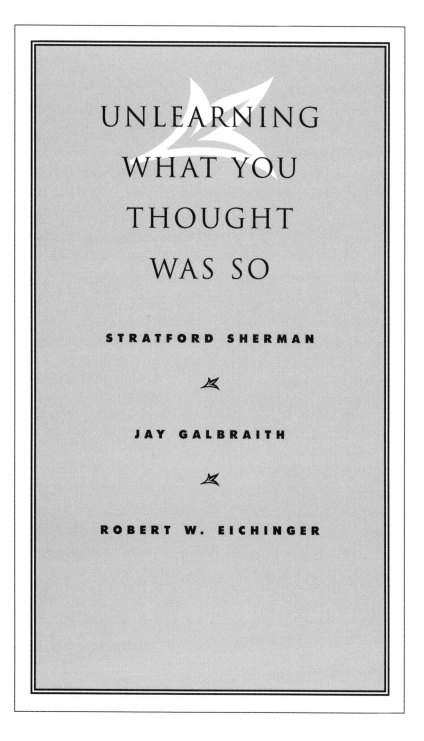

STRATFORD SHERMAN

JAY GALBRAITH

ROBERT W. EICHINGER

23   STRATFORD SHERMAN

Stratford Sherman is a globally recognized authority on leadership, competitive response, and large-scale organizational change. After a two-decade career at Fortune *magazine, where he served on the board of editors, and many years as a sought-after speaker, he established an independent practice offering corporate advice and executive coaching. Sherman coauthored the best-selling study of Jack Welch's transformation of General Electric,* Control Your Destiny or Someone Else Will, *and contributed to the recent* Leading Beyond the Walls. *He is a member of the national advisory board of the Peter Drucker Foundation for Nonprofit Management, and chairman and cofounder of Lalibreria.com. Sherman can be reached at mail@nitya.com.*

What Strength Really Means

As I reflect on my life to date, it seems that the single greatest catalyst of personal growth was the process of making up my mind to propose to the woman who is now my wife. At the time of that decision, Meredith and I had been going out for three years. Three years of being in love and breaking up, loving and breaking up—on the whole it didn't seem to be going very well. At the time, I blamed the problem on what I perceived as Meredith's mood swings; I never considered the impact of my own dread of commitment. Eventually I decided we should separate for a while. My intention was to figure out whether to marry her or give her up for good. During those months, I entered a very intense process of introspection. Early on, the fundamental issue became clear: Meredith needed me to change, and change seemed impossible.

During this time of contemplation, I began to trace the origins of my way of life and, in particular, my resistance to change. My father had been a survivor of the Holocaust and a man who placed great emphasis on inner strength. He had raised me with the idea that to be a man, to be strong, was to be unchanging, like a great boulder in the middle of a raging river. The waters might rage, but the rock would never budge. Over time, I became rather accomplished in that method of living.

The benefits included firmness of character and an ability to withstand strength much greater than my own. As a reporter for a major business magazine, I often matched wits with chief executive officers of very large companies, people who ordinarily would intimidate a young person like me. Thanks to my father's gift of firmness, I felt at ease with them instead.

The idea of marital commitment, however, challenged this independent identity. It seemed to represent a tremendous, even intolerable, risk. After all, I knew who I was; if Meredith couldn't find a way to mesh with me, I figured, the result could only be disaster. My concern struck me as quite reasonable. After all, my parents had gotten divorced, and I had grown up amid ample evidence that marriages often fail, and painfully. I also hesitated to lose what had been a neatly compartmentalized relationship with Meredith, in which I was free to adore certain aspects of her nature, while refusing to deal with the aspects that made me uncomfortable.

As I came to recognize what a childish model of relationship this was, I also realized that the main obstacle we faced had nothing to do with Meredith: It was my own terror about what might lie beyond the chasm of change. I had entered the separation with a long, exquisitely detailed list of complaints about Meredith, precisely specifying every attribute that struck me as unbearable, every potential source of the conflict that, I imagined, might inevitably lead us to divorce. When at last I frankly considered the matter, though, I realized that my love for Meredith was absolute. And in the context of that absolute, all the faults that I perceived in her added up to nothing.

The real issue began to emerge: I didn't want a nice person like Meredith to get stuck with a horrible guy like me. Once I finally stopped criticizing her, I had to acknowledge that she was right about my own need to evolve. Each of the issues that she had raised about my behavior began to seem worthy of consideration. Eventually the issue became clear: To marry Meredith, or indeed to be happy even without her, I would have to free myself of the long-festering feeling of being stuck, my stubborn insistence on preserving my every weakness and evasion. This was when, for the first time in my life, I recognized that I actually wanted to change. My love for this wonderful woman and the overwhelming strength of my desire to keep her in my life finally compelled me to launch a frontal assault on the idea that strength is about resisting change. I felt as if the very bedrock of my identity needed to be blown up. So . . . I blew it up.

The day finally came when I called up Meredith, took her out to dinner, and asked her—with what I thought was enormous charm—to marry me. Meredith didn't say yes. Yikes! I'd summoned the courage to go way out on a limb, and she left me there, trembling. After several weeks of testing my sincerity, trembling herself, she accepted my proposal. We have been married now for more than fifteen years. We have two heavenly children. We have shared all the usual agonies and delights. And together we have experienced more happiness than either of us had ever expected of life.

In retrospect, my adulthood began with the decision to commit to change. The way I view the world shifted profoundly: Since then I have understood that strength of character is the ability to change when change is needed.

Not only my inner life but my professional life has blossomed as a result. From the time I was a boy, I had (like many members of the baby boom generation) been powerfully attracted to the idea of change—so long as it involved other people. Only after I began to experience change myself did my counsel begin to have value, and that value seems to have increased with time. Some years ago, I coauthored a book about the transformation of General Electric under Jack Welch. That work led to my active engagement in the dynamics of organizational transformation as a speaker, consultant, and executive coach. Over time, I have increasingly focused on the way large-scale organizational change interacts with, and depends upon, change at the very personal level of individual employees. Knowing something about change from within my own life has helped me deal with that issue, not as a theory, but as a living reality.

Today I try to help people in leadership positions understand and respect what people go through when they are asked to change. I am convinced that organizational transformation is not only a triumph of leadership but also the sum of individual acts of voluntary commitment. People need to understand their own need for change and decide independently that change is what they want. Without that commitment, shared by a great many individuals, organizational change can't reach beyond the narrow confines of reengineering. That's why I believe it is imperative that leaders understand what their employees want, what they believe, and how they feel. At work, as in marriage, voluntary commitment is the key to success.

QUESTIONS

⚔ *What is it that you're absolutely committed to?*

⚔ *How willing are you, in your own life, to change when change is needed?*

⚔ *Has your experience of change been reluctant and superficial, or has it been deep enough to strengthen your sense of ease and well-being?*

⚔ *In your relations with other people, are you honoring their need to make their own choices freely and without coercion?*

24 JAY GALBRAITH

Jay Galbraith is a professor at the International Institute
for Management Development in Lausanne, Switzerland.
He is on a leave of absence from the University of
Southern California, where he is a professor of manage-
ment and organization and a senior research scientist at
the Center for Effective Organizations. Before joining
the faculty at USC, he directed his own management
consulting firm. Previously, he was on the faculty of the
Wharton School at the University of Pennsylvania and
the Sloan School of Management at MIT. The author of
numerous books and articles, he is currently completing
a new book on global organizations.

Learning to Live with Questions

I was not so much affected by any one incident or event as
I was by a teacher who truly influenced how I think and question.
I'd gone to engineering school, and I was a chemical engineer.
Dissatisfied, I then went to graduate school, where I studied quantitative subjects such as economics, statistics, operations research,
computers, and management. In graduate school I was also
exposed to some nonquantitative disciplines. I took a course with

James D. Thompson, who at the time was writing *Organizations in Action,* a landmark book for people involved in organization theory. In class each week, he would share a new chapter, and we would discuss the ideas it inspired in us.

Most of my professors were people who were selling their subject. I had a professor who was teaching Skinner's reinforcement theory, and according to him, this not only was the best way to understand reinforcement, but it was the only way. Thompson was different. The importance of a question to Professor Thompson lay not so much in delivering an answer but in the question itself. Unlike other teachers, Thompson would rarely answer the questions I came up with. Instead, he would clearly define what the question was and proceed to explore two or three positions that could be taken. The answer to my question was much less important to him than having me truly understand the question. This approach shaped my view on the world.

I was inspired to learn that the purely technical and quantitative answers weren't very satisfying. I understood that they are not what the world's problems are solely about; there is something more human. In my dealings now, I try to put several viewpoints together in an effective package that can help solve a problem. I don't produce a single answer on an issue.

These days I like to stay on the edge, questioning my own ideas and beliefs, whatever I hold as true. I like to look at complex issues and, as a result, often wind up arguing with my clients, who usually want to keep it simple. Sometimes the seduction of simplicity is just that—a seduction. Complexity can be intimidating, but by understanding what the questions are, a framework can be constructed to successfully deal with the issues at hand.

I have also learned to live with a question that has resulted from my research and consulting in organizations. During a consultation, I conduct interviews with the participants, and I have been struck by how partial their views are. They generally see only their part of the organization. After synthesizing a few interviews,

I usually have a broad view of the company. This process has always reminded me of the story of the three blind men, each of whom was aware of only the part of the elephant he could touch. I used to think I could see the whole elephant. But today I ask whether I can see the whole elephant or whether I am one more blind man.

QUESTIONS

🖎 *Are there multiple viewpoints you can access in forming plans?*

🖎 *Do you question your own perspective occasionally and try to see things from another perspective?*

25 ROBERT W. EICHINGER

Robert Eichinger has over thirty-five years of experience teaching, consulting, and working in corporate positions. He now runs his own leadership development product and publishing company, Lominger Limited, Inc. Eichinger is a frequent speaker and workshop leader for companies, associations, and professional groups. He has coauthored a number of articles on executive development, was on the adjunct staff of the Center for Creative Leadership, and codesigned the Leadership Architect® suite of management and executive development tools, which is being used at over five hundred companies worldwide. Retired from active consulting, Eichinger is now running and designing additional leadership development products for Lominger Limited, Inc.

True Learning Is Often Slow

For some reason, I grew up a professional critic. I was good at finding fault with the projects and programs of others, at poking holes in their balloons. As a matter of fact, I still am. I had some classic debates with some of my instructors in college. I guess I thought I could get my head higher if I could make other people's lower. I was bright and brash, and it wasn't that my criticisms were necessarily wrong; they were just constant and overwhelming.

Moving straight out of graduate school and into a consulting firm in Houston, I found myself in my first real job. Full of vigor and book learning, I was ready to change the world. About six months into this new job, my boss, who would be an important mentor to me later, called me in for a six-month review. "Bob," he said, "you are obviously bright and talented. Someday you might make a good consultant. But for now, we would appreciate it if you would keep your criticisms of what other consultants are doing inside the firm to yourself. Frankly, you have no credibility with us yet. You have no right to criticize anyone because you haven't done anything yet. You have come up with about ten good ideas since you have been here. Pick one. Do it. Make it a success. Then we might be interested in what you have to say about the ideas of others. In the meantime, shut up and do something. And by the way, if you can't take something and make it work, your time here will be short."

The principle I needed to learn? He who criticizes must be willing to put himself on the line first to gain the right to criticize others. I did pick something. I made it a success. I curtailed my criticisms and stayed with this consulting firm for eight years. Interestingly, my need to criticize others diminished.

Nine years later, I was corporate head of management development in a Fortune 500 company. My boss called me in one day and said, "The chairman wants to have a leadership model for the company. Go find one." I was excited! This would be my first real exposure to the chairman. I did my homework: I read all the relevant literature, established benchmarks, and went to a leadership conference. I chose the top ten leadership models available at the time and created a great presentation. I had slides (forty-five altogether!) for each model. Method? Author(s)? Findings? I knew them. I had a group of summary slides on the common elements of the ten models and how they differed. I was versed in the pros and cons of each. Rehearsing, I thought, "This is a good piece of work." My professors would be proud. I was ready to go.

My boss was a hands-off type. He didn't want to look at what I had put together before we presented it to the chairman. I didn't sleep the night before. On the day of my presentation, in the boardroom no less, I began with a brief introduction. I described Kotter's model, then went on to Bennis. I was about to go on to Bass when the chairman said, "Bob, is the rest of your presentation like this? Are you going to tell me your opinion of what the leadership model should be for this organization?"

I froze. I looked desperately toward my boss for support. Nothing. I replied that I had read all the literature and was presenting what I had found so that he (the chairman) could decide what he wanted for the company. He said, "I could get a review of the literature for a lot less money than I'm paying you. I want to know what you recommend. I'm not interested in how you got there. If you want to continue working here, have that ready next Wednesday at 3 P.M." He got up and walked out of the boardroom nine minutes into our scheduled hour. "That wasn't a very good start with the chairman," my boss said flatly. Quite an understatement, I thought. He then added, "It's time to put up or shut up. See you next Wednesday."

I went back to work. This time I talked to a number of leaders in the organization about what they thought they needed to be successful. I met with the head of strategic planning to see what she thought the organization was facing in going forward. I talked to my boss about what he thought. Then I went back to my research to find the model.

Synthesizing all of the new information, I came up with eleven factors or "competencies." I defined each of them, performed a "Why might this factor be important around here?" analysis, and again was ready to go. Wednesday came. This time I had fifteen slides: two introductory slides, eleven for the eleven factors, one on why the plan I was proposing would work, and one conclusion. I gave my presentation. The chairman made one change in one of the factors, then said, "Good work. Implement the model." And we did. It was used in that organization for the next eleven years. I stayed for seven more years. The principle I learned? Be a person who adds value. Parroting, no matter how academically sound, isn't of value in the real world.

Eight more years passed, and I had a very hands-on boss. He wanted to see all my work. He was a very good organizational politician, which meant that I and others on his staff seldom got into trouble because he always had useful input; he would edit and rehearse and add value to our work. He and I developed the first enterprise-wide employee survey. My task was to put together the questionnaire. I read the literature, set benchmarks, talked to some questionnaire vendors, interviewed the eight general managers to see what information they needed, and created a questionnaire.

Then a crisis emerged—my boss announced he was leaving. We had the party and said our good-byes. The survey was scheduled to start in two weeks, and the new boss had just come in. I scheduled some time with her. I told her I needed her to review and approve the questions so we could go to print. She said, "If I need to review the questions, I don't need you. If you can't design a survey that adds value and works, I'll get someone else who can." This was becoming a very clear message.

I went back to look at the questions myself. There's no doubt I had become lazy with my previous boss because I knew he would catch any gross political errors. I had put in some questionable items that were of interest to me but that I was sure he would challenge and probably take out. I took most of those out myself. I had two colleagues look at the items, made a couple of changes, and implemented the questionnaire. It was successful and is still being used today, with some new items added each year. The principle I learned this time? Stand up and be counted; be as self-sufficient as possible; do complete work the first time.

These lessons span eighteen years—too long, I suppose, but I am a slow learner. It took three shocks to my system, but these lessons are now firmly embedded in my mind:

1. Add value to everything you do.

2. Be as self-sufficient as possible in what you do.

3. Form a viewpoint on key issues. Stand up and be counted!

4. Criticize sparingly.

QUESTIONS

⚔ *What does it mean to add value?*

⚔ *What does it take to form a viewpoint on an issue?*

⚔ *Why is it important to criticize sparingly?*

PAIN IS A
GREAT TEACHER

MARSHALL GOLDSMITH

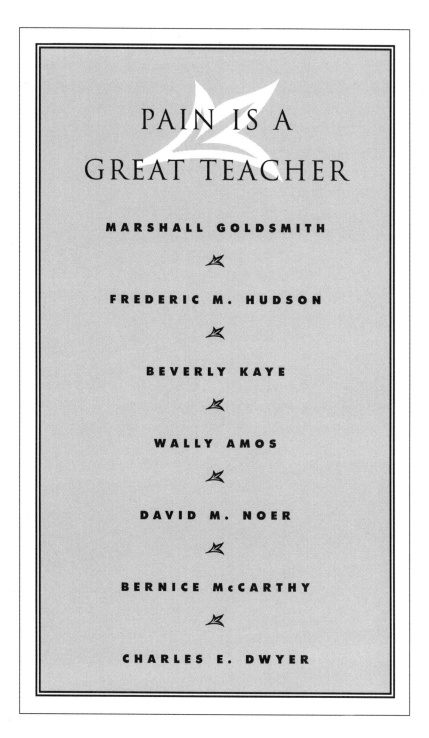

FREDERIC M. HUDSON

BEVERLY KAYE

WALLY AMOS

DAVID M. NOER

BERNICE McCARTHY

CHARLES E. DWYER

26 MARSHALL GOLDSMITH

Marshall Goldsmith is one of the world's foremost author-
ities on helping leaders achieve positive, measurable
change in behavior for themselves, their people, and their
teams. He is executive director of the Financial Times
Knowledge-Leadership Dialogue, a cofounder of Keilty,
Goldsmith & Company, and a member of the board of the
Peter Drucker Foundation. In 2000, Marshall was listed
in Forbes *magazine as one of the top five executive*
coaches and in Human Resources *magazine as one of*
the world's leading HR consultants. He also has been
ranked in the Wall Street Journal *as one of the top ten*
executive educators. Marshall has coauthored or coedited
nine books, including The Leader of the Future *(a*
Business Week *"Top 15" best-seller),* The Community
of the Future *(ranked #1 in its field by Amazon.com),*
and the newly released Coaching for Leadership.

The Person in the Mirror

As a Ph.D. student at UCLA in the early 1970s, I had a
self-image of being "hip" and "cool." I believed I was intensely
involved in deep human understanding, self-actualization, and
the uncovering of profound wisdom. Early in my Ph.D. program,
I was one of thirteen students in a class led by a wise teacher, Bob
Tannenbaum. Bob had come up with the term *sensitivity training,*
had published the most widely distributed article to appear in the

Harvard Business Review, and was a full professor. He was a very important person in our department at UCLA. He is also a great guy.

In Bob's class, we were encouraged to discuss anything we wanted to discuss. I began by talking about people in Los Angeles. For three full weeks I gave monologues about how "screwed up" people in Los Angeles were. "They wear these $78 sequined blue jeans and drive gold Rolls Royces; they are plastic and material-istic; all they care about is impressing others; and they really do not understand what is deep and important in life." (It was easy for me to be an expert on the people of Los Angeles. I had, after all, grown up in a small town in Kentucky.)

One day, after listening to me babble for three weeks, Bob looked at me quizzically and asked, "Marshall, who are you talking to?"

"I am speaking to the group," I answered.

"Who in the group are you talking to?"

"Well, I am talking to everybody," I replied, not quite know-ing where he was headed with this line of questioning.

"I don't know if you realize this," Bob said, "but each time you have spoken, you have looked at only one person. You have addressed your comments toward only one person. And you seem interested in the opinion of only one person. Who is that person?"

"That is interesting. Let me think about it," I replied. Then (after careful consideration) I said, "You?"

He said, "That's right, me. There are twelve other people in this room. Why don't you seem interested in any of them?"

Now that I had dug myself into a hole, I decided to dig even deeper. I said, "You know, Dr. Tannenbaum, I think you can understand the true significance of what I am saying. I think you can truly understand how 'screwed up' it is to try to run around and impress people all the time. I believe you have a deep understanding of what is really important in life."

Bob looked at me and said, "Marshall, is there any chance that for the last three weeks all you have been trying to do is impress me?"

I was amazed at Bob's obvious lack of insight! "Not at all!" I declared. "I don't think you have understood one thing I have said! I have been explaining to you how screwed up it is to try to impress other people. I think you have totally missed my point, and frankly, I am a little disappointed in your lack of understanding!"

He looked at me, scratched his beard, and concluded, "No. I think I understand."

I looked around and saw twelve people scratching their faces and thinking, "Yes. We understand."

Suddenly, I had a deep dislike for Dr. Tannenbaum. I devoted a lot of energy to figuring out his psychological problems and understanding why he was confused. But after six months, it finally dawned on me that the person with the issue wasn't him. It wasn't even the people in Los Angeles. The person with the real issue was me. I finally looked in the mirror and said, "You know, old Dr. Tannenbaum was exactly right."

Two of the great lessons I began to understand from this experience were (1) that it is much easier to see our problems in others than it is to see them in ourselves, and (2) even though we may be able to deny our problems to ourselves, they may be very obvious to the people who are observing us.

There is almost always a discrepancy between the self we think we are and the self the rest of the world sees in us. The lesson I learned (and strive in my professional work to help others understand) is that often the rest of the world has a more accurate perspective than we do. If we can stop, listen, and think about what others see in us, we have a great opportunity. We can compare the self that we want to be with the self we are presenting to the rest of the world. We can then begin to make the real changes needed to align our stated values with our actual behavior.

I have told this story at least three hundred times, and I have thought about it more frequently than I have told it. Often when I become self-righteous, preachy, holier than thou, or angry about some perceived injustice, I eventually realize that the issue is not with the other person or people. The issue is usually in me.

Today I work mostly with executives in large organizations. I help them develop a profile of desired leadership behavior. Then I provide them with confidential feedback, which allows them to compare their behavior (as perceived by others) with their profile of desired behavior. I try to help them deal with this feedback in a positive way, to learn from it, and (eventually) to become a good role model for the desired leadership behavior in their organization. Although I am supposed to be a "coach," very little of my coaching involves "sharing my wisdom." Most of it involves helping my clients learn from the people around them. In this way, the lesson I learned from Bob Tannenbaum has not only helped me in my personal life; it has helped shape the course of my professional life.

QUESTIONS

- ⚔ *Can you see in yourself what others see in you, or do you see in others what you don't want to see in yourself?*

- ⚔ *What really bothers you about the "rest of the world"?*

- ⚔ *Is there a chance that some of your concerns may be a reflection of your problems, not theirs?*

- ⚔ *How can honest feedback from others help you in aligning your values with your behavior?*

27 FREDERIC M. HUDSON

*Frederic Hudson is an educator, writer, trainer, and rec-
ognized adult change expert. He is widely respected for
his contributions to the fields of adult development, career
transition planning, and human and organization development. As a Rockefeller and Danforth Fellow, Hudson
earned his doctorate at Columbia University and taught
at Colby College and the University of San Francisco.
From 1974 through 1986, he was the founding president
of the Fielding Institute. In 1987 he founded The Hudson
Institute of Santa Barbara, a training center focused on
coaching and renewal in the workplace and for the individual. Hudson was named "Executive Coach of the
Year" by AT&T, "The Best Seminar Leader We've Ever
Had" by 3M, and "Life/Work Balance Coach" by
Harley-Davidson. He is author of* The Adult Years:
Mastering the Art of Self-Renewal.

My Wake-up Call

My life course was shaped indelibly by a traumatic event
in my childhood. I share this story here because it vividly represents the message of my life: always have a vision, formulate a
plan, and lean into the wind.

On August 23, 1943, when I was nine years old, I awakened in
silent terror. I was unable to move any part of my body except my
eyes. My muscles seemed frozen, and my voice was silenced.

Although I had gone to bed as a walking, talking, wiggling boy, I woke up the next day paralyzed with polio. Neither my legs nor my arms would respond to my desperate efforts to move, and my neck and jaw were as rigid as rocks. My breathing was panicked, and I felt pain everywhere. In the 1940s, polio was a dreaded epidemic of unidentified origin for which there was no means of prevention and no real medical treatment. Many who contracted it died; others went through life in braces and wheelchairs.

The next thing I remember was lying on the backseat of my parents' car as they drove me thirty miles to a hospital in Syracuse, New York. That journey was unbelievably painful. I was sicker than I had ever felt in my life, and I felt a helplessness and fear I had never experienced before. "What will happen to me?" I pondered. "Am I going to die? Will I ever see my family again? It isn't fair!" That day remains vivid in my mind, like a screeching siren I can't turn off.

At the hospital, I was placed on a very hard bed with no pillow, in a quarantined ward. I spent my waking moments staring upward at the ceiling—my only option—feeling totally helpless.

A wise nurse named Susan spent lots of time with me. Quiet and caring, she visited me frequently and told me many things. Her main message was something like this: "Your future, Frederic, is hidden on the ceiling, and you are the only one who can find it. Look for what you will be doing as you grow up. It's all up there. Will you be a track star, a tennis player, a scientist? Will you be going on trips to faraway places? Will you be going to summer camps and swimming? Will you go to college and become someone special? Will you marry and have a family? Frederic, all you have to do is study the ceiling. When you see your future, it will start to happen!"

That's all she ever talked about—my future. I spent hours and then days and months searching for snapshots of my future in the maze on that dirty ceiling above my immobile body. The first vision I saw had me running and playing and active again. I saw myself as a young deer leaping effortlessly through a forest. After a while, I had only to lift up my eyes and I would see myself bouncing along, alive with graceful movements and amazing speed. Then I saw myself having friends, laughing again, and climbing trees. After a few months of ceiling gazing, I pictured myself going to college and becoming a husband and father someday. I even envisioned myself as a doctor.

Susan convinced me that if I would keep rehearsing my vision on the ceiling, sooner or later my body would begin to move again and make it all happen. I never doubted her. At the very time when my body was at its all-time low, I trusted her to coach me toward my highest self. Knowing my eyeballs were my only moving part, she brought a projector into my room and flashed stories and pictures on the ceiling for me to consider as I pondered my future. She projected a checkerboard and taught me how to play checkers and chess as she facilitated a learning environment for my future. She would read me books while instructing me to find my life in the patterns overhead. She brought me music to listen to, as well as recordings of famous books. Slowly but surely I began to feel the world of sound and sight open up before me.

She obtained my school assignments for the fourth and fifth grades and tutored me without my even knowing I was doing schoolwork. Honoring my wish to become a medical doctor, Susan procured the graduate bulletins of Yale, Harvard, and Columbia medical schools. She deciphered the undergraduate prerequisites and modified the learning process to suit someone my age. Before I left the hospital, she had engaged me with advanced mathematics, French, philosophy, and English literature. I felt so privileged to be learning so much that I imagined that everyone in my class was in a hospital somewhere—with polio—learning from nurses like Susan!

Before contracting polio, I had not been much of a student. My family was struggling to survive the Depression and World War II, and I was squeezed in between a brother a year older and a sister a year younger. Life was a day-by-day scramble. My father worked in a pharmaceutical manufacturing plant, and my mother worked part time as a clerk in a drugstore.

But during my months in the hospital, in my desperate physical condition, time was all I had, and I wanted to learn everything I could. I wanted to become everything I could become. And I believed that what I envisioned on the ceiling would come to pass. Everything I imagined seemed possible, and what did I have to lose? Except for me, the room was silent and empty. I had no radio, and TV had not yet been invented. Thank God! It took a lot of silence for me to find my soul and invent my future.

One day, as I was entranced in a forest walk along the cracks in the ceiling, I felt a wiggle in the toes of my left foot. It was not much, but it was everything. I could move my toes, a little. When Susan made her rounds, she assured me that this was the beginning of my future unfolding, not merely my getting well, but my visions being realized. She said my strength would slowly return up my legs, my backbone and arms, and finally my upper neck and chin. "You are now in training," she would say, "so practice moving your foot for the rest of the month." She tied a string to my toes up through an eyelet she screwed into the ceiling (I winced when she made a hole in the secret garden of my mind's eye), and secured a small bell to it. "Ring the bell," she insisted, and I did, having no knowledge of Pavlov and his dog.

I was astounded that Susan knew the path to my recovery and transformation. She placed twine around my foot, up through a pulley (screwed into the ceiling!) and down to a handle on a casement window to my right. "Frederic," she whispered, "make the window go open and closed until it makes so much noise that every nurse on the floor scolds you." This was high motivation for a nine-year-old, and although I was unable to move my foot for weeks or months, my attention was completely riveted to doing so. In time, it happened, and only years later did I learn that all the nurses were instructed by Susan to rush into my room to complain royally.

In time, my room looked like a gymnasium, with ropes going in various directions to engage my awakening limbs with necessary exercise. I loved my room, and I had no intention of ever leaving. As ugly and bereft as it was, it was my secret garden. Never before had I been so awake, alive, and ready to soar. The last parts to cooperate were my neck and upper chest, and although I still can't touch my chin to my chest, I have been eternally grateful for everything I learned and became in my recovery. I now walk, run, play tennis, and live without any noticeable deficit.

The hardest thing I ever did was leave that room. I cried in anguish as my wheelchair left the hospital for my uncle's farm, where I was quarantined to learn to walk again. My loneliness there was punctuated by the deadly, daily visits of an orthopedic nurse who made me exercise, without any of the mentoring Susan had provided. It was months before I could walk, but when I did, I had a vision of where I was going and how I would get there. I had a purpose, and I planned my life around it.

I did not fully grasp what Susan had taught me until midlife, when I was struggling mightily with my path and my life course. By then I had shifted from becoming a doctor of medicine to becoming a doctor of philosophy. After earning a Ph.D. at Columbia University, one of the schools Susan had recommended, I became a professor of philosophy at Colby College in Maine and then at the University of San Francisco. I also became a husband and a father. I wrote some books, became a good public speaker, and arrived at the goals I had envisioned with Susan.

In my late thirties, when my youth felt spent, I thought my life was over. I was out of vision. After much soul searching, I returned to what I had learned from Susan—to be visionary and responsible for my own future. Since I remained Susan's close friend until her death in 1989, I phoned to get her advice. This is what she said: "Yesterday's dreams are not always tomorrow's promises, Frederic. Gaze at the sky above you as if you were in the hospital again, and get a new fix on where you are going, and why.

What we need at midlife is not always what we wanted when we were young. Find the fire, the passion, the hope that belongs to you. It's always up there, ready to be loaned to the right person at the right time." I cried with joy.

So again I learned, painfully, to gaze at the ceiling of my life to find new paths into my future. I tell my story so every reader can benefit from Susan's simple wisdom:

- Envision how you want your life to unfold.

- Look for your best choices.

- Trust your vision. All anyone has is time. Make the most of it.

- Create a detailed plan to get you from here to there.

- Take responsibility for your life course: Time manage every detail.

- Find the best resources available for empowering your future. Network, train, travel, seek, adventure.

- Learn how to learn, unlearn, and relearn. Make learning your central business.

- Live on the outer edge of your reach, not on the inner edge of your security.

QUESTIONS

Gaze at your ceiling. What do you see for yourself?

What actions can you take to get there?

How can you play the role of Susan and help others gain a vision?

28 BEVERLY KAYE

Beverly Kaye is president of Career Systems International, Inc. Her management and career development programs are used by such corporations as American Express, Dow Corning, Chevron, Chrysler, Marriott International, and Sears. She is a prolific writer, popular lecturer, and management consultant. In the early 1980s, Kaye published her now-classic book Up Is Not the Only Way. *Her latest research is on management strategies for retaining knowledge workers, and she has recently coauthored* Love 'Em or Lose 'Em: Getting Good People to Stay. *Kaye has received many honors and awards, including the National Career Development Award of the American Society for Training and Development. She earned a doctorate at UCLA and did graduate work in organization development at the Sloan School of Management at MIT.*

Making the Flat Side Round

Kirkegaard had it right when he said that life must be lived forward but can only be understood backward. I translate this: If only I had known then what I know now! One incident that changed my view of myself and gave me the platform I still stand on today almost proved to be my own undoing.

It happened at UCLA. I had completed my coursework and had to defend my dissertation. My subject was organizational career development. I had selected a committee I thought knew me, liked me, and would be gentle. I had also selected, as was my style, a dissertation approach I could get my arms around. It would be relatively clean, clear, quick (I hoped), and something that would fit my style, which was "take action," "move quickly," "work hard," and "check it off the list"—a Jersey girl approach.

As I now understand backward, my learning style was limited. I memorized thoroughly, studied long and hard, and did everything I could to get extra credit. I didn't see myself as naturally smart, and therefore everything took more time, more pain. But I was a diligent student and knew what to do to get through. I knew my learning comfort areas and boundaries.

And unfortunately, my committee knew them too.

My dissertation approach was rejected. I had been so sure of myself that I had been taping it for my folks. The committee told me to start again and described the approach I should take. I now had a cassette filled with my begging them to reconsider and not "do this to me at the END of my education."

That, of course, clinched it for them. And for me.

They asked me to do phenomenological research: grounded theory. They said they saw my flat side; I operated from my intuition and not from a theory base. I didn't know what they were asking me to do, but I was sure I would not like it. And I didn't, not one bit. Nor did I have any idea how to do it, even though I read Glaser and Strauss's *Grounded Theory* several times.

Phenomenological research requires that you develop your own theory. You investigate a phenomenon and collect data. When your theory holds all your data, you've got it. Three times I tried. Three times I struck out. Sitting with data was just not me. Sitting and thinking was just not me. *Sitting* was definitely not me!

Two things kept me going: My mom (when she saw how upset I was) said, "Why not quit?" (and then I knew I couldn't), and one of the professors on my committee said, "Bev, if you hang in there, this will be your career development." I didn't know what that meant, but I knew it was an important message.

I finally got smart. Out of desperation (and loneliness), I hired a friend to sit and listen to me talk about the data I had collected. As I talked and as she listened, the theory began to bubble up. And when I presented my findings, the committee finally said, "By George, she's got it!"

That theory became my first book; that book led to my consulting practice and to the tools and materials I have since developed both on my own and with colleagues. That theory, now updated, is with me today in all I teach, and in all I teach others to teach. It still guides my thinking; it grounds me and directs me.

So what did I learn? I learned that I needed to be pushed out of my comfort zone to really learn what I could do. I recognized that I was caught in what David Kolb would term two and only two learning styles: "active experimentation" and "concrete experience." If I were ever to truly develop, I had to add "reflective observation" and "abstract conceptualization" to my bag.

I've often thought that if the committee had described it to me that way, I might not have fought it as I did. If they had drawn that learning cycle and explained how this was going to "round me out," I would not have suffered so much. I would have known where they were trying to help me go. Maybe.

I learned that if one is to have a platform, one has to come to that platform in one's own time and in one's one way. And when it is truly yours, you stand on firm ground. From that firm ground, you can do almost anything.

I learned that collaboration (for me) is sweet, that my best thinking is done in concert with others, and that there is nothing wrong with asking for help. I've used that lesson to grow my business, my practice, and my approach to living.

I learned (and have had to relearn more than once) that it is when the ground turns to quicksand that the most valuable learning and most valuable and enduring growth is about to happen. Oh, that there were an easier way!

QUESTIONS

- *Who or what has pushed you and caused you to grow and develop in new directions? How?*

- *What is your flat side? How can you be more well-rounded?*

29

WALLY AMOS

The founder of Famous Amos Cookies, Wally Amos has used his fame to support educational causes and to inspire others to adopt a positive outlook on life. His new company, the Uncle Noname Cookie Company, has received critical acclaim. A nationally sought-after inspirational lecturer and author, Amos is also a television host on PBS. He has received the Horatio Alger Award and the President's Award for Entrepreneurial Excellence. Among his four books is an autobiography, The Famous Amos Story: The Face That Launched a Thousand Chips. *Amos has been a spokesman for Literacy Volunteers of America since 1979.*

Ten Lessons on Bouncing Back

Personal and professional ruin once stared me in the face. But I managed to triumph over financial misfortune because I drew on the power within to turn a seemingly hopeless situation into an absolute winner.

I have learned that crises can turn out to be glorious benefits if we draw on universal wisdom to handle them. And problems, or challenges as I call them, are valuable catalysts for our personal growth.

I believe our imagination is the source of our individuality, our capacity for glory, and our own peerless talents. I use the creative power of my mind to confront and shape my unique reality because I know my vision involves me emotionally in my activities. I love and enjoy everything I do because I see my projects and experiences as an extension of myself. This total investment accounts for my success. Your own dreams and goals will become a reality to the extent that you pour yourself into them.

Everyone who has achieved greatness or fulfillment in life started out with a dream. Prayer and visualization call up your limitless spiritual resources to move you toward your vision. In meditation, I let my imagination run rampant. Once I have dreamed my final goal, I construct mental pictures of the steps leading to the goal. Then I go out with a heart filled with passion and actualize what I have seen.

Total commitment to your cause is like throwing a pebble into a lake; it creates ripples of value and good fortune. Worthy results inevitably follow. And if you have boundless enthusiasm for the task at hand, you invigorate everyone around you and inspire them to take up the challenge even in difficult times. Your faith in the outcome will enable you to bounce back.

When I was forced out of my own company, it seemed utterly unfair. But while it looked like my brainchild had chosen to betray me, my intuition told me a divine plan was at work. I meditated and reminded myself that life is a process in which everything works for the best. I knew I was not a victim. Finally I came to a place of understanding. My suffering and rejection turned into a sense of comfort and peace.

I was once asked to outline the principles that helped me through my crisis. Here they are:

1. *Don't become part of the problem.* I was faced with an extremely unpleasant situation, but I did not internalize

the dispute and defend myself in a combative manner. I undertook to concentrate on the worthwhile things in my life and turned over the lawsuit to a trustworthy professional. In short, I focused on answers and solutions that were within my grasp.

I focused on my new role. I centered myself on principles and decided how I could conduct myself. This provided the framework of my future. I followed through by doing something every day to get myself a little bit closer to achieving my goal. There is an internal peace that comes from giving your all and looking at life from a positive angle.

2. *Accept and acknowledge the reality of your situation.* In my situation, I realized that nothing could change the facts: Wishing the crisis away would not help; getting angry and yelling would not help; and denying that there was a problem would only make it worse. I had to tell myself that the course of events did not depend entirely on me. I could turn this lemon into lemonade, or I could let it sour my whole life.

3. *Remain committed to creating a new life for yourself.* Even through the darkest and most depressing times, even when I privately thought things could not be worse, I still woke up each morning determined to stay the course for as long as it lasted. I really had no choice. I had to redeem myself and take care of my family, so I had to keep my heart and my mind completely on track. I never gave up. I either had to swim toward solutions or sink and lose everything.

4. *Allow the experience to open you up to what you need to learn.* Every situation is an education. I once had a habit of spending a lot of energy explaining myself and my course of action to other people. I was not wise or secure enough to hear their ideas. I preferred being right to being happy. I learned that if you open your mind to the voices of

others, you will open your life to receiving good. They say there is a reason why God gave us two ears and one mouth: We should listen twice as much as we speak! I enhance my chances for growth and achievement as I learn to overcome my ego.

5. *Maintain a positive mental attitude.* A positive mental attitude is the basis of my philosophy of life. Positive people have positive effects on the world around them. W. Clement Stone says the ultimate secret of success is to keep your mind on the things you want and off the things you don't want. It is as simple as that. Regardless of the appearance of a situation, there is always good to be found. I make sure I seek the beauty and wisdom in everything, and believe it or not, I always find it.

6. *Hold on to your faith.* The noted Princeton professor Cornel West has an astute way of describing strong faith. He says, "Faith is stepping out onto nothing and landing on something." When we have faith, we reinforce our subconscious to make our lives move forward and flourish. We create our own circumstances, and our subconscious merely reproduces in our environment what we conjure up in our minds. Vitality, luck, love—everything comes to us as we draw such qualities out of ourselves.

7. *Consciously practice living in the present.* It always helps me to be mindful and aware of each moment so I can make the best use of the time I have. If I had wasted my energy on thinking what could have gone wrong with the lawsuit and how it could have turned out, I would have inhibited my ability to live each day effectively. If you live in the moment, you will realize you have everything you need to deal with your life. The past cannot be changed nor the future predicted, but each moment in the present is a building block to creating a happy existence. I take care not to reflect on the past or project into the future; rather, I believe it is the present that counts. "Do it now!" is my motto.

8. *Keep your sense of enthusiasm alive and active.* Enthusiasm creates joy. Joy creates more joy. Maintaining a joyful outlook and keeping a high level of enthusiasm can sometimes be difficult, but the more you do it, the easier it gets. The rewards always reflect what you invest.

9. *Engage in acts of selflessness.* Throughout the nineteen months of the lawsuit, I still made time for my charitable and nonprofit activities. Even if it is the last thing I am able to do, I will still devote myself to giving. I've been blessed with benefits both immeasurable and incredible. Not only did I receive emotional and spiritual support from my literacy and dropout prevention work, but I also ensured the success of my business by establishing myself in the heart of a community of people who came to my aid when I needed them.

10. *Aim at responsibility, honesty, and integrity at all times.* We are all part of the whole, and however we act determines what we receive. There is a law of cause and effect, and what we express comes back to us faithfully. I want the very best for myself, my family, society, and this world. I realize that I can set my sights on that dream only if I am prepared to live my life in an honorable fashion with every action I take.

I take care to follow these principles. I give the best of myself, and I get the best in return. Lemonade, anyone?

QUESTIONS

⚔ *Why are failure and adversity such good teachers?*

⚔ *What can you do to turn a painful experience into a positive one?*

⚔ *What has adversity taught you?*

30 DAVID M. NOER

*David Noer is an author, a researcher, and a consultant.
He has written six books and numerous academic and
popular articles on the application of human spirit
to leadership. He heads his own consulting firm in
Greensboro, North Carolina, where he specializes in
helping organizations and people through transitions by
harnessing the power of applied human spirit. He has
been designated an Honorary Senior Fellow of the Center
for Creative Leadership and was previously senior vice
president for training and education with worldwide
responsibility for the center's operational, training,
licensing, and educational activities.*

The Gain Is Worth the Pain

The great teachers of my life gave me a precious gift. It
was not a tool, process, or technology; it was something deeper and
more profound. They helped me understand that what really matters when helping people or organizations through change and
transition is not technique but authenticity, vulnerability, and
empathy. They taught me that connecting with others at the
warm, messy, and unscientific level of the human spirit is a

prerequisite for any methodology or process. I learned that technique without a grounding in empathy and vulnerability is sterile and artificial. I learned, as Larry Porter, one of my many great teachers, once said, "In the final analysis, the only tool worth a damn is our own warm body."

Larry's message has been reinforced and expanded by a number of other great teachers whose messages also reside in a unique and shadowy portion of my mind. Internalizing what they have been telling me has not been easy. I was, and at times continue to be, a resistant student. I grew up conditioned by dust bowl empiricism, where the operating theory was, "If you can't measure it, it doesn't exist." Unfortunately, this early tenet of the natural sciences has been adopted by many of the applied behavioral sciences, and it does not always support their effectiveness. My great teachers talk about concepts such as love, trust, vulnerability, empathy, and authenticity. "Try measuring those!" they shout in unison from their residence in my mind. "Empathy first, methodology second," they cry in rebuke whenever I become enamored of the latest gimmick or flavor of the month.

I've been lucky to have discovered many great teachers in my life. Collectively, they have helped block my tendency to escape from authenticity into technique. The magic part about my relationship with these teachers is that they are always there when I need them. There are many of them, and I don't always know who is on duty until she or he emerges. Some are well known, and others are not. In my experience, not all great teachers have fame or visibility, and not all well-known management gurus are great teachers. Some of the most famous are only a conduit for a single technique or methodology. They are solutions looking for problems.

My voyage of discovery began years ago when I was promoted to senior vice president of a large financial services holding company. Human resources was one of the functions that reported to me, and I found myself on what proved to be a "mission impossible." I wanted to drive out arbitrariness, hidden agendas, and power politics to make the organization more effective and people more creative and empowered. One of my great teachers emerged: Tony Tasca, who with his unique blend of humor and Sicilian worldliness introduced me to the basic values and processes of organization development. Through Tony, I was introduced to Pat Williams, who was just starting the Pepperdine MSOD program. As the founder and designer of the Pepperdine program, Pat has shaped the lives and perspectives of OD practitioners for more than twenty-five years. Pat and his late colleague Dave Peters taught me that the more in touch you are with what makes you tick and who you are, the more effective you will be in helping both people and systems change. I went to Pepperdine looking for a tool kit, and left with the dawning realization that I was the tool! I also discovered that as a tool I needed some calibrating and honing. You can only take someone as far as you've gone yourself.

My quest for external technique, however, still simmered and led me to the doctoral program at George Washington University. Maybe there I would find the right set of tools and methodologies. Instead I found Peter Vaill, another member of the growing cadre of great teachers whose messages live in that special corner of my mind. Peter, along with his colleague Jerry Harvey, taught me that knowledge and wisdom often take paths that resist measurement and control. I emerged from George Washington in midlife with a newly minted doctoral diploma and the increasing belief that dropping my defenses and establishing an authentic relationship with those I was attempting to help was of much more value than keeping control and applying objective tools and processes to management issues. It isn't that objective, external tools and techniques are bad or not useful; the point is that they are applied to human systems, and they require a context of authentic human interaction to work.

Life has a way of keeping us humble, and I was hit between the eyes with a large dose of humility in 1988. I had just left my well-paying corporate job and had accepted a lower salary for a more interesting faculty position at Duke University. Two weeks before I was to start, my wife, Diana, broke her neck in a car accident. Luckily she survived, albeit with some permanent damage, but not nearly as bad as what we anticipated at the time. I was thrust into a caretaker role and couldn't move to North Carolina and was therefore out of a job.

In this time of spiritual, emotional, and financial need, three great teachers emerged. All three gave me the same message: I knew more than I gave myself credit for, and if I stayed authentic and truly focused on the client's needs, as opposed to a methodology or technique, I too could be a great consultant and teacher.

The first lessons came from Dick Leider, who helped me get clear on my sense of purpose and bolstered my sagging ego and self-esteem by simply declaring me a "great spirit" and a "truth teller." He convinced me by providing the analytical part of me with concrete examples to support his declarations.

The next two lessons came from Dick Byrd and Marshall Goldsmith. They both brought me into consulting assignments with nothing to go on but trust (theirs, not mine) that I could do the work. "You know more than you know you know. Quit trying to analyze it and just do it!" said Dick as he thrust me into a complex and confusing client group. Marshall phoned from California, expressed his concern over Diana's accident, and asked what I was going to do. "I think I'll try consulting, but I don't have any clients," I said. "What are you doing next Tuesday?" asked Marshall. I didn't have any pressing engagements, so I joined him in Atlanta to work with one of his clients. That was it: no references, no letters of agreement, no conditions, no doubts (again from Marshall, not me). The kindness, faith, and unconditional optimism of both Dick and Marshall not only caused my declining self-esteem to soar, but also taught me the power of a positive self-fulfilling prophecy and reaffirmed that the currency of the realm in a helping relationship is applied human spirit, not method or technique.

As I look back on what I have accomplished and learned, I am grateful for the many teachers whose lessons live within me and deeply appreciative of their magical ability to materialize when I need them the most. They have helped me understand that help is in the perception of the person receiving the help, not of the person giving it. I have learned that technique and method are important but always need to be applied within the context of an authentic human relationship. My great teachers continue to help me understand that method, no matter how technical or complex, is easy. The hard part is dropping my defenses, being vulnerable, and establishing an authentic human connection.

QUESTIONS

- *If you are trying to lead, manage, or consult, have you gone through the necessary pain, struggle, and self-analysis that will allow you drop your defenses, become vulnerable, and engage with your fellow humans (be they employees, bosses, or clients) in an authentic manner?*

- *Are you able to differentiate between the objective, predictable, and essentially nonhuman arena of techniques and methodologies and the subjective, warm arena of authentic human interaction, where transformation that can empower the soul and make the human spirit soar is possible?*

31 BERNICE McCARTHY

Bernice McCarthy is president of Excel, Inc., an educational consulting firm headquartered in Barrington, Illinois. She is the creator of The 4MAT System, which frames a natural cycle for designing learning at all levels, for enhancing communicating, teaming, and problem solving, and for honoring the diversity of all learners. McCarthy earned her doctorate in education from Northwestern Unversity in 1979. She founded Excel, Inc., that same year and has continued as its president throughout the history of the company. Her most recent book is About Learning.

How Truth Can Lead to Falsehood

There was a time several years ago when I had worked hard to convince a group of my fellow teachers that we needed to change the way we structured our high school. My goal was to create an environment in which all children were able to thrive, especially those who were performing poorly in the current academic setting.

We worked for months on a plan for structuring the school to create an environment in which all students could learn. We wanted to provide students with more ways to express their knowledge, more ways to take responsibility for their learning, and more ways to make connections between what they were learning and its real-life impact. We formed a committee and created what we believed was a workable design, and finally we were ready to present our recommendation to the entire faculty. I was to be the spokesperson.

I addressed the group, explaining our plan, and everything went very well. It soon became clear that we were going to get exactly what we were recommending. Everyone on the committee breathed a sigh of relief. Just at that point, one of the members of my own committee stood up and suggested a change in the program. I was horrified! I could not believe he wanted to add another dimension to the structure at that point in the process. In fact, he wanted to make it possible for students entering the school to have the option to choose the traditional curriculum that was already in place. After all of our hard work to design what was clearly a superior approach, and just as we were on the brink of getting full approval, my colleague wanted to give students the option to keep things the way they'd always been!

My reaction was instantaneous. I had been betrayed. Where in the world was he coming from? I wanted to wring his neck. Then the realization of what I was feeling hit me. I was so enamored of my own idea of how the new system should work that I was in danger of losing everything I had championed. I had become rigid in my thinking, the very thing I had fought so hard to change in others.

It was a telling moment for me, and the memory will always stay with me.

All real change involves major uncertainty, and we cannot deny the questioning time to others simply because we have already answered the questions for ourselves.

When we become good at what we do and enjoy success, we are in danger of believing our way is the best and our perceptions the best ones. In the process, we sometimes lose sight of what matters most: the interplay of ideas and the active engagement in life.

We need to find the courage to expand our world while allowing others to find their own truths. We need to invite opposition among those with differing viewpoints. While it is not always possible for me to do so, I have become better at honoring the skeptics in my audiences. I try to see them as passionate people who can add richness to the dialogue. I can use their comments now to help me ponder and grow, and I have become more aware of how truth can lead us to falsehood if we stay in love with our own ideas.

The experience on the curriculum committee was a wonderful learning experience. It taught me to be open to dialogue with others, while trusting my own values and insights.

QUESTIONS

⚔ *When presenting ideas to others, are you more interested in winning them over or in hearing what they think?*

⚔ *When you are absolutely sure of something, ask yourself, "What if the exact opposite is true? How would this change my thinking and my course of action?"*

32 CHARLES E. DWYER

Charles Dwyer, Ph.D., has been on the faculty of the
University of Pennsylvania since 1966. He is academic
director for the Aresty Institute's Managing People
Program in the Wharton School. He is also an associate
professor in the Graduate School of Education. Dwyer
has more than thirty years of experience in educational,
corporate, and organizational consulting. His client list
includes IBM, Dupont, Xerox, MCI, Bell Atlantic,
Westinghouse, R.J.R./Nabisco, and others. His research
and teaching cover a wide variety of topics, from
interactive planning to group processes and personal
development.

What Do You Do When
Things Go Wrong?

Many years ago, I designed a program for the Wharton
School called "The Effective Executive." It consisted of two
weeks' worth of material and we gave it all over the country, usually in resort settings. We'd offer one core week and then several
iterations for the second week. Anybody who took the first week
was eligible to take the second week at a different location and a

different time. In the early days of this program, I taught four of the ten days and recruited other people from the Wharton School to take on other topics.

Early in the program's history, one of the participants, to whom I am forever grateful, came to me and said "This is not going well at all." I was a little surprised by this, because I had screened the presenters for the program very carefully. They were often award-winning teachers in the university. He told me what he thought was going wrong with the material and my colleague's presentation.

It was a very difficult situation. On the one hand, I had some very unhappy participants; his report was not just of his own dissatisfaction. I discovered there were many people in the group who were dissatisfied with what was going on that morning. I came back in after the break with the faculty member who was making the presentation and said, "You know, we're going to have to hold it here. I understand there are some real issues; things aren't going well." And he said, "Well, I sensed that."

I asked him to step aside. I was the director of the program, and I had to take responsibility for what was (and what was not) going on. Even though my stomach was in my throat I stood in front of about forty people, all executives and high-level managers in corporate America. As comfortably and calmly as I could, I said, "I understand that things aren't going well. Can you give me some details?" The place erupted. I allowed them time to vent: the time they had given up, the money they had given up, this wasn't what they had expected, and so on.

I said, "Fine. Here are some alternatives for the rest of the week, and I want you to choose among the alternatives or tell me other things that you want me to try to do in the next few days." I broke them into small groups, had them discuss outcomes, and had a reporter and recorder appointed to each group. When they came back together, they presented a series of suggestions to the planning group.

As stressful as this event was, it was a deep and valuable learning experience. It was emotionally difficult for me, not only as the primary presenter in the program, but also as the person ultimately responsible for the quality of the program and the satisfaction of the participants. On top of this was the fact that this was one of Wharton's offerings. There was a great deal in terms of image that had to be upheld. Word of mouth is often the most powerful way to get people to subsequent programs, and the program was being offered several more times that year. I could have easily panicked, but I didn't. Why, I don't know. I didn't get defensive, and I didn't rationalize the situation. I took it at face value and said I'm the one responsible, and these are the clients. Let's find out what they want and what's going wrong here and how we can fix it.

What was incredible was how positive things were from then on. This experience showed me that if you don't get defensive and don't rationalize, you are able to listen to people and they will be reasonable. You are then able to respond to their input. After that experience, I've commented to people on occasion that I've almost been tempted to make something go wrong within this kind of setting and then "make it right" for the goodwill that comes from the participants. I could imagine walking into the room calmly and saying, "Okay, folks, not everything always goes right in our lives."

The personal impact this experience had on me gave me a strong level of confidence when things go wrong. I now have a way of reacting to the unexpected; I know what that way is and I know that it works. Will it work in all situations? Probably not. However, there have been two or three situations, perhaps not as dramatic and intense as this example, in which my plans didn't go right, and I didn't swallow my stomach. I was calm because I knew what steps I was going to take and what the power of those steps was likely to be. And the difficult situation always turned around.

The other important outcome of this experience is that I don't worry about things going wrong. There's a certain level of concern in all of us when we're up in front of the room. You're a little bit like the pitcher in the ball game with everybody staring at you, and you either strike them out or you don't. I no longer feel that level of negative pressure to perform, because I know now that I can switch from pitching ideas to catching ideas when the plan needs to be changed.

QUESTIONS

⚔ *What do you do when things go wrong?*

⚔ *What checks can you put in place for yourself to gauge your effectiveness?*

MENTORS
MATTER

RICHARD J. LEIDER

LOU TICE

CHIP R. BELL

ROBERT FRITZ

JOEL BARKER

33

RICHARD J. LEIDER

Richard Leider is a founding partner of the Inventure Group, a corporate training firm devoted to helping individuals, leaders, and teams discover the power of purpose. As a pioneer in the field of life/work planning, Leider has become an internationally respected author, speaker, and career coach, as well as a noted spokesman for "life skill" for the twenty-first century. He has written four books: The Inventures, Life Skills, Repacking Your Bags, *and* The Power of Purpose. *He leads annual Inventure Expedition walking safaris in Tanzania, East Africa.*

Does All That Make You Happy?

An "inventure" expedition is an adventure within yourself. To inventure is to have the courage to look inside and discover your essence. Since 1983 I have led inventure expeditions to different places within the same regions in Africa. On one of my early inventures, we were backpacking in a corridor along the eastern edge of the Serengeti Plains. It was the first day of the trip, and our guide was a Masai chief by the name of Koyie. He and two of his warriors knew the area, and we were to camp with them at various villages along the way.

This was my first experience with Koyie and his first experience with anything like the people in our group. During our trek he carried nothing, and I carried a large, oversized pack containing a first-aid kit and lots of camping "necessities" as well as my own personal items. Throughout the day's hike, I labored under the weight of my pack, and Koyie could see the effort I was expending under this burden.

We finally arrived at our destination. Tired, I threw my pack down on the ground and waited for the elder of the village to greet us and give us permission to stay there for the night. Koyie couldn't stand it any longer. He came over to me and very politely asked if I would show him what I was carrying. So I unloaded my pack and, object by object, shared the contents, including the bottles in my first-aid kit, Ziploc bags, Gortex, rain gear, and velcro—all the important things we take for granted that he had never seen before.

I had plenty of gear because we were going to be away from "civilization" for a while, and it took me a full ten mintues to unload the pack. Curious to see this spectacle, the entire village gathered around me to observe. Like Koyie, they had never seen anything like this before. Koyie, who had been watching patiently, looked at me, surrounded by enough products to stock a small dry goods store, and asked very simply but with great intensity, "Dick, does all this make you happy?"

I was stunned. There was something very powerful about Koyie's question. His words hit right at the heart of my deepest values. Immediately defensive, I said, "Well you know, I planned for this trip; I'm the leader," and I explained why I needed each item. Then I quickly stuffed everything back into my pack and went to my tent to collect myself. But I had been given a blinding glimpse of the obvious: I didn't need everything I was carrying. In a split second, Koyie's question had forced me to think about all I was carrying and why—not just on the trek but in my entire life.

I returned a short time later to the dozen or so people who made up the group and told them I was going to leave half of my things with the villagers. This prompted others in the group to start talking about what they were carrying. What is interesting, however, is that almost immediately the conversation shifted to our personal burdens and choices. What weights do we carry in our work lives and in our relationships? What journey are we on, and what do we need for that journey?

My load was much lighter after I'd reexamined my needs, and on the rest of the trip, I was happier for having repacked my bags. What Koyie helped me to do is what I now try to help other people do through both outdoor and indoor adventure. When people put down what they're carrying, look at what is inside, and determine the essentials, they are able to identify the essence of who they are. Once that essence is identified, the individual can pack accordingly for the journey ahead.

QUESTIONS

🖎 *What's weighing you down?*

🖎 *What would help you lighten your load?*

34 LOU TICE

Lou Tice is chairman and cofounder of the Pacific
Institute, an educational corporation that operates on
six continents and is based in Seattle, Washington.
He is the author of Smart Talk for Achieving Your
Potential; A Better World, A Better You; *and*
Personal Coaching for Results, *with Joyce Quick, as*
well as the creator of the video best-seller Investment in
Excellence®. *Before founding the Pacific Institute with*
his wife, Diane, in 1971, Tice worked as a high school
teacher and football coach. For nearly thirty years, he has
been in the business of helping people and organizations
reach their potential.

Mentoring for Untapped Potential

Most successful people have had at least one significant coach or mentor in their lives. What does a good mentor do that a role model doesn't? Think about it. Who have your mentors been? What did they do for you?

I'll bet they were people who could see more in you than you saw in yourself at the time. They saw you not only as you were, but also as you could be. They had a vision for you that was probably bigger than any you had for yourself. They weren't blind to your shortcomings and flaws, but they didn't focus on them. Instead, they helped you believe in your own strength, ability, and potential for growth. They inspired you and helped you to see possibilities for your life that you may not have seen otherwise.

Because your mentors had credibility in your eyes, you gave sanction to their visions. Then your self-talk followed suit: "Yes, that is possible for me. I could do that. I am like that." Your beliefs about yourself changed, and you began to act differently. Great coaches and mentors are so unshakably convinced that we have greatness in us, and their vision of what is possible for us is so clear and powerful, that they wind up convincing us, too.

MY FIRST MENTORS

I don't know where I'd be today if it had not been for the influence of people I looked up to who believed in me, especially those who were there for me when I was a kid. Sometimes I imagine the worst: I see myself as an aging, alcoholic football coach, mad at the world because I couldn't help anyone, even myself, to be a winner.

Then I think of Mr. Anderson, my sixth-grade teacher. He was a wonderful role model and mentor for me. He routinely put me in charge of the class at recess—a big responsibility—which made me feel like a capable leader. When he organized team sports, he sometimes put me in to play instead of more experienced, older players, even when those guys protested. I reasoned that I had to be worth it. Mr. Anderson had credibility in my eyes, and he made me believe I was someone special. So I made sure I behaved as if I was. I was determined that I wouldn't disappoint him or let him down. He went out of his way to set up experiences for me that reinforced my belief in myself, and I will always remember him for that.

I will also remember Evan Thomas. Evan was three years older than I, and we grew up in the same miserable neighborhood.

Because of the heavy production demands of World War II, none of the kids where we lived had much adult supervision. Parents who were lucky enough to have jobs were putting in as many hours as possible, often working extra shifts. Older kids were pressed into service to care for younger ones. As a result, we often ran wild.

But Evan was different. He was physically, mentally, and morally strong. He was a Native American, but he didn't set himself apart from the rest of the kids. We thought of him as one of us but somehow better. You can imagine how it felt to have him notice me, to single me out, and to care enough about what happened to me to give me advice. When he told me to avoid certain people because they weren't good for me, I listened.

Evan was a fullback and a starter on the high school football team. I had always wanted to play football, too, but when I reached the ninth grade I was still small for my age, so I went unnoticed by the coach among the hundred or so boys who showed up for tryouts. I was sure I'd never make the team, but Evan wouldn't hear of it. "Here's what you need to do," he told me. "Don't let the coach out of your sight. You just go and stand by him every day, and tell him you want a uniform." I would never have dreamed of doing this on my own, but if Evan thought I was good enough to deserve a uniform, I figured it must be true. So I did what he suggested, and my persistence paid off. The coach gave me a uniform, and that's how I made the team.

The first time I went out with Diane, my wife, we double dated with Evan and his girlfriend. I was going to take Diane on the bus, but that wasn't good enough for me, according to Evan. "You'll go with us in my car. I'll pick you up, and then we'll pick up Diane," he told me. "But what if this girl you're going out with doesn't want us along?" I asked him nervously, remembering that they were three years older. "Don't worry about that," Evan said. "If she doesn't like it, we'll just leave her home. You're my friend." Again, he made me feel important at a time when it mattered.

I heard that Evan died from a brain tumor about fifteen years ago. I was very disturbed by the news and especially disturbed that I had never told him how much his friendship and support had meant to me when we were kids. So I decided to talk to his mother. I drove across town to the old neighborhood and found the Thomas house.

Mrs. Thomas didn't remember me at all, but I told her what a fine person Evan had been. I explained how deeply he had influenced me and how important he had been to my growth, my character development, and my success in life. I told her that his attention and concern had meant the world to me at a time when I was in need of those things, and I told her how proud I had felt to have been Evan's friend. I told her I would never forget him, and I never will.

AFFIRM THE GREATNESS YOU SEE

The most powerful act any of us perform for others is to help them access their untapped potential, help them nurture and grow the best parts of themselves, those aspects that are hopeful, brave, persistent, inquisitive, hardworking, creative, resilient, kind, assertive, thoughtful, and resourceful.

What is our potential as human beings? No one knows, but we haven't even begun to approach our limits. Potential means capable of being, with a capacity for development. When we help others to value and believe in themselves, when we help them to feel supported in their choices no matter what the outcomes may be, we help them to grow into their greatness.

Saying that we shouldn't try to solve other people's problems or stand between them and the rightful consequences of their actions doesn't mean that we should do nothing. As mentors, we can offer much in the way of experience and wisdom. For instance, through skillful questioning, we can help people clarify the elements of a problem or decision they are thinking through. We can help them identify and evaluate their options and then create scenarios for various courses of action, imagining the outcomes of each. We can point out possibilities they may have missed and suggest alternatives. We can share our own strategies and the results of similar experiences that we have lived through, both successful and unsuccessful. (Sometimes our failures, mistakes, and aborted attempts can teach far more than those times of relatively smooth sailing.)

When we're sure we understand a situation, we can propose constructive actions or behavior changes—as long as we accept that our protegé is free to agree or disagree, to accept or reject our proposals, and as long as we don't disapprove or feel disappointed if our ideas are questioned or rejected. We can help others examine and adjust their self-talk, especially their affirmations and visualizations, and know themselves better. And we can help them review and evaluate the consequences of their decisions and what new decisions need to be made as a result of those consequences.

QUESTIONS

✘ *How can you be a better mentor to someone you live with or work with?*

✘ *What can you do to help another person reach his or her potential?*

✘ *What questions can you ask to help clarify the elements of a problem or decision someone else is working through?*

35 CHIP R. BELL

Chip Bell, a senior partner with Performance Research Associates, manages the company's Dallas, Texas, office. An internationally known speaker and consultant, he is the author or coauthor of twelve books, including Managers As Mentors, Customers As Partners, Instructing for Results, Understanding Training, Dance Lessons: Six Steps to Great Partnerships in Business and Life, *and* Beep Beep: Competing in the Age of the Road Runner .

Seven Lessons on Teaching and Training

"He was the best teacher I ever had." That was something I heard often when I was growing up. The subject was my father; the fan club was populated by his former high school students. By the time I reached adulthood, I too had joined the "Ray Bell's a Great Teacher" fan club.

Ray Bell was never my teacher in the formal sense of the word. By the time I arrived on the scene, he had left the teaching profession to become a full-time banker and full-time farmer. But the teacher in him never got turned off. Consequently, I was the lucky student of his tutelage. His influence changed my life. His wisdom provided valuable touchstones for my life's work as a trainer.

Here are the basic precepts of the Ray Bell approach to teacher training.

1. *Great teachers are judgment free.* My father could be a stern taskmaster and a tough disciplinarian. He was very much a perfectionist when it came to performance. He expected the best, demanded the best, and demonstrated the best. However, when the goal was learning, he shifted to a completely different style. He suddenly became patient, even tolerant, and above all, nonjudgmental. When the objective was growth, he would treat the most inane question as a query reflecting insight just waiting to happen.

   He never snickered at my ignorance or scorned my naiveté. As a young man, I was much more likely to hear "Good try!" than to hear "Good gracious!" If I was busy working to acquire new skills or knowledge, leeway and latitude seemed to be his specialty. Great teachers are quick to confirm and slow to correct. They use body language that speaks acceptance and affirmation. They suspend critique, knowing judgment impedes risk taking and experimentation, both necessary for effective learning.

2. *Great teachers are participative partners.* "How 'bout going and getting the tractor and parking it in the barn?" Those sweet words were music to my ears when I was a ten-year-old growing up on a farm. It was Dad's way of nudging along my maturity. To get the very special privilege of starting, driving, and parking a large, expensive tractor was to feel trusted and respected. Dad's gesture made me feel thrilled and tall.

The tractor-parking incident was more than a badge of being grown up. It was a symbol of partnership—I obviously relied on Dad, but at that moment, he trusted me enough to return that dependence. Great teachers perpetually seek ways to include and to partner. They would rather facilitate than lecture; they enjoy great questions more than smart answers. Dad joined in the pursuit, offering guidance, not expertness. He seemed to know that participation was the route to discovery and insight, an important building block for significant learning.

3. *Great teachers show perpetual curiosity.* My father asked me questions to which he did not know the answer. This trait always stood in stark contrast with what I witnessed in many of my friends' parents. My buddies frequently were asked questions with the slam of a spring-loaded bear trap. "Do you have any idea what time it is?" was not an "I lost my watch" kind of question. But Dad never used questions that way. When he asked a question, it always meant he was in search of an answer. I came to realize it was evidence of his perpetual curiosity.

   On family driving trips, we stopped at every historical road sign. We had long Sunday afternoon discussions provoked by queries such as, "What do you reckon Charles Dickens meant by that?" or "I wonder what Julius Caesar might have been feeling when that happened?" He took things apart just to see how they were made. He watched squirrels build a nest and then launched into a question-filled discussion of nest-building genes or weather-sensing skills. Great teachers never stop being curious. They view themselves as learners more than teachers. And they are both passionate and unabashed in their nonstop inquisitiveness.

4. *Great teachers find humor in most situations.* Dad was no comedian. In fact, he was a very shy man. But he enjoyed a great tease and was as quick to laugh at himself as he was

to laugh with others. His humor was innocent and authentic, never contrived or sarcastic. Most important, he saw lightness in simple occurrences and enchantment in ordinary events. When he laughed, his expressions were bounteous and unbridled; his declarations of joy were always contagious.

He intuitively knew that merriment was a key piece in the puzzle of learning. When learners encounter humor and joy in their teachers, they learn to laugh at themselves. The serious pursuit of growth must be coupled with an unserious process of growth. Ray Bell demonstrated that no matter how grave the destination, the trip needed to be a pleasurable one. He was the only teacher I had who could find a whimsical side to trigonometry or to Charles Dickens. The by-product of his example was my gaining an unerasable fondness for learning. That path has enabled me to become more and more a self-directed learner, learning simply for the joy of the trip.

5. *Great teachers show obvious pride*. Ray Bell experienced life firsthand. But he also experienced life secondhand. When my hard-earned competence was displayed in a public presentation, it was as if he too were on the stage, down the court, across the field, or in the pulpit. He was noticeably proud of the accomplishments of his children. And his pride never had a possessive "That's *my* boy," credit-seeking dimension. He simply seemed to be thrilled to see how it all worked out.

Great teachers are proud to witness the effects of their teacher-learner relationships. They not only vicariously experience the growth of their learners, but they also look for ways to bear witness to the power of learning. Dad's sense of "Isn't that great!" or "Isn't that amazing!" was not an expression of surprise that I could actually do what he taught me. Rather, he was awed by the process of learning.

6. *Great teachers have impeccable ethics.* The most important lesson I learned from my father was that teaching is an ethical act. Effective teachers and trainers must be clean in their dealings with learners, not false, manipulative, or greedy. Good teachers are honest and congruent in their communications and actions. They never steal their learners' opportunities for struggle or moments of glory. They refrain from coveting their learners' talents or falsifying their own. Good teachers honor the learner just as they honor the process of mutual learning.

7. *Great teachers have great love for their students.* Ray Bell was all about love, and it infused his teaching relationship. When his former students spoke of their fond memories, it was clear they were speaking of someone they loved and of one who loved in return. Dr. Malcolm Knowles taught me that a good teacher or trainer must first and foremost love the learning. Ray Bell taught me an even deeper lesson: a great teacher or trainer must first and last love the learner.

QUESTIONS

- *If your learner were to give you a grade based on your own enthusiasm for learning, what grade would you get?*

- *In your learning or training programs, what would better equip participants to be more effective, lifelong learners?*

- *What role have you played in awakening the senses of your learners? What made them blush? What made them giggle?*

36 ROBERT FRITZ

For more than twenty years, Robert Fritz has been developing the field of structural dynamics through his work related to the creative process as well as organizational, business, and management issues. He is the founder of Robert Fritz, Inc., Technologies for Creating®, Inc., and the Fritz Consulting Group. He is cofounder of Choicepoint, Inc., producer of the management software Stuctural Tension Pro™. Fritz is the author of five books, The Path of Least Resistance, Creating, Corporate Tides, The Inescapable Laws of Organizational Structure, *and* The Path of Least Resistance for Managers. *An active composer, Fritz has written film scores, operas, symphonic music, and chamber music, and he was on the faculties of the New England Conservatory of Music and Berklee College.*

Pushing Through to the Next Level

When people realize my background is in music, they ask me how a conservatory-trained composer became interested in organizations and business. For me, learning to learn came directly from my study of music. Their questions always make me think of one of my music teachers, Mr. Poto.

A HARD LESSON

Attilio Poto was a member of the Boston Symphony Orchestra, a faculty member of the Boston Conservatory of Music, and a marvelous clarinetist. My first few lessons had to do with physical changes in my technique and my choice of curriculum. Mr. Poto decided that I would use a very difficult book of etudes, one I knew was well beyond my ability. I suggested an easier approach, but Mr. Poto said he had his reasons for the choice. So that was that.

The first week's etude was very difficult for me. I worked hard to perfect it, but I just couldn't play it very well. When it came time for my lesson, I tried to play the assigned etude, but I made many mistakes. Mr. Poto made suggestions and showed me how to play certain passages. I commented that I should spend another week practicing this piece, as I knew I needed more time and experience. As I was telling him this, Mr. Poto simply smiled at me and turned the page to the next exercise, one that was even more difficult than the one I had struggled with the previous week. I thought Mr. Poto wasn't a very good teacher.

The next week's lesson was terrible. Try as I might, I made even more mistakes, and my performance of the etude was dreadful. I was sure this time that Mr. Poto would give me another week to get it right. But instead he flashed his sweet smile and turned the page. "Don't you think another week . . . ?" He didn't. Poor man. He may have been a master clarinetist, but as a teacher . . . .

Week after week was a repeat of the same pattern. I worked hard and couldn't play very well, but Mr. Poto just assigned me more difficult etudes. Finally, after six weeks of this torture, Mr. Poto taught me the real lesson. I began my usual complaint of "I can't learn this way," when Mr. Poto smiled and turned to the very first etude I had had such trouble with weeks before. "Play it, please," Mr. Poto instructed. I did. In fact, I played it well. The earlier difficulties had disappeared. Now I could do everything that had seemed impossible six weeks before. I played the piece much better than if I had spent the entire six weeks practicing that one etude.

Mr. Poto turned the page to the next etude. Again I could play it. It felt easy. With the third etude, it was the same story.

The lesson that Mr. Poto taught is still with me: The time to move ahead is before you think you are ready to move ahead. This is quite a revolutionary principle in light of our usual educational practices. Generally we believe that we must perfect something before we move to the next step. Moving ahead before you think you are ready is often uncomfortable. It feels wrong. It is counter-intuitive. But all disciplines feel uncomfortable at first, because the physics of discipline involve doing something that is unnatural. It is natural to scratch when we have an itch. It takes discipline to not scratch.

It is not natural to learn how to ski, for example. The ski instructor says, "Lean down the mountain." But the new skier wants to lean away from, not toward, the bottom of the mountain. The way skis are designed, we are able to put on the brakes and control our speed only by leaning down. When we lean back, we "floor it," speeding up with less control than we would have otherwise, especially if we're beginners.

Discipline may not be natural, but it is the triumph of choice over instinct. With discipline, we are able to accomplish more than our instincts would ever allow. Therefore, make the choice to move ahead just before you think you are ready. That way you will assimilate the lessons you have been learning. Not only that, but you will create momentum that helps the learning process. Learning becomes easier and easier, even if what we are learning becomes harder and harder. This approach takes a high tolerance for being less than perfect at first.

THE SPIRIT

Another profound lesson I learned at the conservatory was also the result of an early experience with a teacher—this time one of my composition teachers. Early in the term he gave me an assignment. I quickly knocked it off and brought it to the next lesson. I gave it to him, and he began to study it. For several minutes the room was very quiet as he contemplated my work. Finally he said, "This is very good." I felt pleased and self-satisfied. Then he added, "But I know you're capable of more. And unless you are willing to reach for that, don't come back." I was shocked. But the feeling was more complex than simple shock. I felt found out, and I felt relieved that I was found out. Here was a teacher who wasn't fooled by my talent and natural ability. He was in the business of helping me reach my potential, not in the business of massaging my ego.

The level of commitment underlying my learning mode changed in that moment. "Do a good job" was replaced by "Reach for that which is highest in you." This was one of the best lessons I ever learned.

Learning in a vacuum rarely leads to the kind of profound discipline it takes to reach beyond ourselves into new worlds of ability and experience. Like building muscles, development doesn't happen all at once. It happens over time that is spent in the realm of the unfamiliar, disorienting, and perplexing. How high do we reach, what are our values, and what is the essence of our character? Discipline is the key, and aspiration is the spirit in learning that enables us to extend beyond our limits to reach our dreams.

QUESTIONS

How might you supply "music lessons" to others?

Have you ever tried moving ahead before you have attained perfection?

Can you reach a little more and try a little harder in your efforts?

37 JOEL BARKER

*Joel Barker is a noted futurist whose videos about para-
digms have influenced the thinking of people worldwide
about leadership. In 1975 Barker pioneered the application of paradigm shift theory to organizational vision.
He also invented and refined tools that help reveal the
long-term implications of change. Since the early 1980s,
he has worked with most of the Fortune 500 companies
and many other major institutions around the world. He
is the author of* Paradigms *and* Future Edge, *which was
listed as one of the most influential business books of 1992
by* Library Journal. *Barker's company, Infinity Limited,
Inc., is based in Minneapolis. His most recent videos are
found in the Paradigm Mastery Series.*

Lessons from My Coach

Most of us count ourselves lucky when we have the chance
to spend a year under the tutelage of a great teacher. I was lucky
enough to spend five years with Evar Silvernagle, the finest high
school swimming coach I could have asked for. My time with him
began when I was on the swim team in the eighth grade. I was big
and strong for my age and by midseason I had broken every school
record for my age group.

One day as I was getting ready for practice, Coach Silvernagle walked in. He came over to me, introduced himself in a soft voice, and said, "I would like you to join the A squad, starting tomorrow." And then he left.

Me on the varsity team? I was overwhelmed. My teammates came over and congratulated me. What an honor! The next day I showed up for practice and Coach Silvernagle introduced me to his team. This team came from a long lineage of swimmers who over the past six years had not lost a swimming meet, including state championships, and had produced more than two dozen All-American swimmers. And this was in Rochester, Minnesota, a town with a population of less than 30,000. Coach Silvernagle concluded his introduction of me by saying, "We expect great things of Joel."

And so began my education by Coach Silvernagle. Now, let me give you the punch line first, so that there is no suspense. I never got any faster than I was in the eighth grade. I never earned a letter in the sport. But I stayed on the team for five years because of the greatness of Coach Silvernagle. He taught me lessons that I have used throughout my life. His leadership changed the way I related to the world. Here are the most important things I learned from him.

First, always be inclusive. Coach Silvernagle never cut anyone from his team. All the teams we competed against typically had twenty to thirty swimmers. I was never on a Silvernagle team smaller than sixty swimmers. The coach had a very simple philosophy: If you were willing to do the workouts, he always had a spot for you, no matter how slow you were. With that many kids in the pool, it should have been impossible to produce a good team, much less a state championship team. But he did, year after year.

Second, never stop experimenting. Coach Silvernagle was always trying to learn new ways to teach the strokes, new ways to execute dives, new ways to set up the workouts. He would start by saying that he had an idea, that he wasn't sure it would work, but would we be willing to try it? And then he would draw us into the experiment and ask us what we thought about it after we were done. And he always listened carefully to our answers. Whatever worked we applied with a vengeance.

Third, never give up on anyone. Remember that I never got any faster. Wouldn't you think he would have figured out that I reached my peak and stopped trying to help me get better? Throughout the five years, every time I asked for help, he was there. He never complained; he always gave his time and attention. He acted as if there was always a chance something would change and you would become a great swimmer.

Fourth, excellence is the only target. Here was a man who understood continuous improvement and the purpose of excellence decades before it became a catch phrase in business. He never, and I mean never, talked down another team. Even when the team knew we could shut out the other team, Coach spoke of the opponent with the greatest respect. When he described the match-ups of the various races, he invariably shared with us the other teams' best times, even if they had been achieved last season. Our times were always our most recent. He never talked about beating the other team, only about what our target goals were.

Once the captain of our team bragged to someone that we were going to "kill our opponent" that week. Coach Silvernagle heard about the boast, and the captain was not allowed to dress for the meet. No disrespect was allowed. There was a corollary to this rule: Never underestimate your opponents.

When Coach Silvernagle made up his swim list, it had two versions. Our best swimmers started the meet and swam until we had scored enough points to win the meet. The other team was always honored by having to compete against our strongest swimmers. But once we had the necessary points, Coach went to the second swim list. Our best sat down and the other swimmers got to compete.

What that meant, of course, was that many kids got to swim in the meets. It also meant that the swimmers from the other teams got a chance to take first and seconds. So, in his willingness to give his own swimmers a chance, Coach Silvernagle also allowed the other teams' swimmers to look good. He never ran up the score against weaker teams by continuing to use his strongest swimmers.

For five years I got to watch this man teach boys so much more than how to swim. I watched him teach how to win with honor and lose with dignity. I watched him give respect to the slowest and teach humility to the fastest. Many years later, another great teacher from Rochester gave his evaluation of Evar Silvernagle: "He was the most perfect man I ever met."

By the way, even though I was never more than a mediocre swimmer, I turned out to be a good swimming coach. Those years of instruction did pay off after all.

QUESTIONS

- ✍ *How might you be more inclusive with the members of your teams, your family?*
- ✍ *How might you experiment with routine procedures?*
- ✍ *Are you afraid to let all your team members get in the game?*
- ✍ *What would you really lose by giving everyone a chance to contribute to the team?*

Afterword

The Power of Stories

Many things are so intimate to the human experience that we rarely think about them, such as the wisdom we receive from listening to stories and our ability to laugh at ourselves—two traits that distinguish us from animals. Consider laughter for a moment. While seated with some friends one evening, one individual shared that he had recently taken his nine-year-old son on a meditation retreat. The conversation wandered to how children seem to think they know everything, which prompted me to comment that now that his son had sat at the feet of a guru, he might have gone from being a "smart ass" to a "wise ass." Everyone chuckled. But when I asked the group to reflect on why they had laughed, no one could give a reasonable explanation. I can only wonder at what is encoded in our shared human experience that makes some things funny and others dry and humorless. It is difficult to explain, but undeniable.

The powerful role that stories play in our lives also seems indisputable, but just as mysterious as laughter. They can move us to tears, teach us profound lessons, open up unforeseen ways to understand our lives, and transform our pain into something wondrous. But why? Consider for a moment what it is about the following story that, I hope, leaves you with a smile and a nod of recognition about its inherent truth.

A young man once went to a guru and asked him how he might obtain wisdom. After some thought, the guru responded, "To gain wisdom, my son, you must have good judgment." This response gave the young student something to ponder, but he wasn't wholly satisfied. A few days later he returned to the master and inquired what it would take to attain good judgment, if that was indeed the path to wisdom. Once again, the guru pondered the question, then smiled, saying, "To develop good judgment, you must have a great deal of experience." For a while this answer mollified the young man's curiosity, but seeds of discontent began to sprout. If he needed experience to acquire good judgment, and good judgment to gain wisdom, how could he get the appropriate experience? Once again he approached the teacher. Without hesitation, the wise man responded, "Oh, that is simple. To get experience, you must exercise a great deal of bad judgment!"

In such a simple fashion, stories can convey much that other forms of communication cannot. Some of the world's greatest philosophers have devoted tomes to the subject of wisdom, but I have never heard a more elegant definition than the one in this story. Nor are these philosophers' explanations as accessible to the common intellect. Perhaps this is why we have begun to re-embrace stories at a time when so much of our information sharing is compressed into sound bites and we are bombarded daily by a perplexing glut of data. Stories are an antidote to both, feeding something in us that is hungry for more than bare-bones facts and distilled information, while also making complex ideas understandable and even actionable. Because of a story, people can make remarkable changes in their behavior and overall lives. Large groups have changed the course of history through the unadorned sharing of uncomplicated faith stories. There is something profound and mysterious here, but as natural as breathing.

Stories also give us so much more than a mere lesson. They provide a context, and when we hear a good one, like laughter, they are unmistakable in their impact on our being. In some work I did recently for a major Fortune 500 company around the area of knowledge management, I discovered that the company has devoted much time and money to capturing the lessons it has learned from past projects. Somewhere along the way, top management had concluded that this activity would be important to the long-term vitality of the organization. When completed, the documents pertaining to this project are neatly stored in a library in the company's corporate headquarters. You would think that a place that contains the collective wisdom of the company would be a hotbed of activity and learning, but the opposite is the case. Not one soul has ever gone there! The reason should be apparent: When the lessons of the past are offered without the stories that led to them, it is difficult, if not impossible, for us to learn from the experience of others. If the lessons were all that mattered, then it would be simple to raise children, for example. We'd just give them the manual containing the distilled wisdom gained from the follies of our own youth, and they would adjust their behavior accordingly. The absurdity of such a proposition is evident. But that is in fact what happens in business every day, with equally ineffective results. It also shows up in career development and management books.

By contrast, the stories contained in this volume are so powerful that they inspire us to learn in a way that nothing else can—giving us something precious that we could expect to receive only from a grandparent with whom we have had a long and intimate relationship. When we hear a story, we get to travel vicariously down the same path as the person who first learned from an experience. If the authors in this book had simply told us what they had learned without sharing how they came to these insights, the lessons would be flat, uninteresting, and probably devoid of value. By wrapping the conclusions in the cloak of a story, the lessons become digestible, nourishing our soul as well as our intellect.

As a way to learn, perhaps none understood the technology of stories better than Native Americans. My best teacher in this regard has been Paula Underwood, a descendant of the Oneida people. From an early age, children in her tradition would be taught using this age-old communication tool. Unlike our tradition of fables, in which we tell the story and then tell the reader or listener what the story means, when elders in this learning way concluded the telling of a story, they would gently ask a child to reflect on its meaning. The Oneida understood thousands of years ago that as we listen to or read a story, it is strictly a right-brain affair. It is felt, sensed, and translated into images in our mind. While there may be some learning at this point, it is incomplete. Only when we are asked, "What might you learn from this story?" do we move over to linear thinking in the left brain, teasing out the many lessons that the story holds for us. Marrying these two modes of knowing is what leads to whole learning. Using this simple approach, it is amazing what can be revealed by a mere story. There may be lessons that even the teller failed to see or expect. On the other hand, if we are told what the story means, we are robbed of the opportunity to make these important connections for ourselves, and learning is short-circuited. If you ask this learning question at the conclusion of each story in this volume, you may be surprised by the profound insights and thinking that emerge unaided by the wisdom of the teller.

Stories also refer us to the rich texture of our own experience. In that way, they are soulful. As we hear a story, we find ourselves drawn into our imagination, making subtle associations with past events in our own lives. Stories, like waves from the ocean, wash over us, bringing to the shores of our consciousness rich material from the water's depths, while also washing away sand from the shore to expose layers beneath the surface. You can't hear a story without being delivered to the currents of your own experience, with many related stories being stirred up and emerging into full view.

I also have found it useful to liken learning stories to windows that at times reveal the intricate interior of the experience of people who have traveled difficult roads, and at other times reflect back to us an image of ourselves. When we frame our own experiences in the light of the experiences of others, the reflection often exposes a facet of our own person that was previously obscured or unclear. While houses are similar in many respects, each home is remarkably unique. Likewise, looking into a house through different windows offers different perspectives on the same room. As we proceed with decorating our own interiors with rich textures and furnishings that enhance our lives, it is often useful to see how others have approached the same task. Surely our tastes will differ, and we would never do things exactly the way another would. But you can't help but get ideas of how you might add a little color here, or combine the things you already have in a new and unusual way that is both pleasing to the soul and elegant to the eye. In building our own lives we can't help but benefit from seeing how others have approached the assignment, and learn from their mistakes and their triumphs.

I recently heard Syd Lieberman, a wonderful storyteller, share his definition of humor: "Things are funny when we work our life from the opposite side of the street." Think about it. When we are in the middle of the trials that life so readily dishes up, we rarely have any perspective, and certainly there is nothing funny about our pain or the difficulties we endure. But if we go across the street and watch the unfolding drama through the perspective of time, things often take on a certain absurdity, leading us to laugh and even learn. Why? Perhaps it is because when we see our lives through the prism of a story, it may be the nearest we can come to the jocular viewpoint of the laughing Buddha. That's what I think this lovely volume of stories does for us. It allows us to see with clarity our lives reflected back through the lens of others' experiences. I hope these tales will enrich you as they have filled me with their humanity and wisdom. And, if we take a few steps back, ever mindful of the open manhole as we cross the street, perhaps we will learn the most important lesson of all—to find understanding, and even humor, in the seemingly senseless events, failures, and painful losses that weave their way through our lives.

Richard Stone
Author of *The Healing Art of Storytelling*

Appendix
Resources for Training and Personal Development

We hope that you will want to use the stories in this book to create workshops or interventions that stand on their own in addition to using this book in your own self-development. In this section we offer two training designs that can be used as is or tailored to meet specific objectives. Following the designs are two suggestions to help you take the stories to the next level in your development, personally and professionally.

TRAINING DESIGN 1: DIFFERENCES TEACH

We can learn much about our own thinking and framing of problems by looking at how others approached a situation and perhaps handled it differently than we might have. This design calls upon participants to read a story and then take the story through the "different-from-me" test.

Objective:

- To learn more about our individual approaches to problem solving and confronting life's challenges.

- To gain a greater perspective on alternative routes to confronting difficult situations.

- To differentiate between strategies that might be added to one's repertoire and those that might be too much of a stretch.

For this exercise, ask each group member to select a story from the book in which the author chose a strategy or a path that was different from what the group member would have chosen. Invite individuals to tell the group about their choice. Probe with any of the following questions, or add your own:

- Was it difficult to find such a story?

- Did it jump out at you immediately? What made it jump out?

- What might you have done, or tried to do, if you were in this situation?

- Has this worked for you? How so?

- When has it not worked, or when might it not work for you? Explain.

- What about the strategy this person chose is most unlike you?

- Which part of the strategy seems most difficult now?

- If this strategy were in your current repertoire, what would it enable you to do differently?

- What parts of it seem most viable to you?

- What do you think the individual learned? What would be your own lessons learned?

If time permits, encourage individuals to react to the story from their own perspectives, or ask them to discuss the speaker to gain a fuller sense of their current repertoire in handling this kind of situation and what might be gained by extending it. Closing comments might refer to diversity of thought or style in approaching life's issues, or perhaps to selecting one course of action over another. Participants should record the lessons learned from the story itself and from the discussion as well.

TRAINING DESIGN 2:
TELL ME A STORY

It is sometimes easy to take for granted what we have accomplished during our lives. The stories each of us have to share are powerful learning resources, valuable not only to ourselves but to the people around us. Each of us has experiences that have provided incredible learning. It is important not only to remind ourselves of our own experiences that have brought us to where we are, but also to share our stories with others so they can gain greater insight into who we are both collectively and individually.

Objective:

- To increase the sense of individual empowerment.

- To practice the process of storytelling.

- To bring more cohesion to the group via sharing of personal experiences.

For this exercise, ask the participants to think about the various themes in the book. Suggest that they take a few moments to reflect upon pivotal experiences in their own lives. What stories emerge from those experiences? Ask the group to share as much as they feel comfortable sharing. The point of the exercise is to appreciate the individual learning process and experience and to practice sharing stories with those around you. During this reflective process, ask participants to consider the following questions:

- What did you learn from the experience?

- Why was it important?

- If the story relates to a specific theme in the book, under which theme would it fall?

In bringing this exercise to a close, ask participants what they learned from not only expressing their own story but hearing others' stories. Were people impressed or surprised by what they heard or learned?

PERSONAL REFLECTIONS 1: DISCOVERING THE STORIES IN YOUR OWN LIFE

This is an invitation to capture the living wisdom that comes to all of us in the course of our daily lives. Interesting things begin to happen when you look at your life to discover your own stories. By looking at your life with a sense of curiosity and a spirit of exploration, you will make connections that can provide valuable insights into yourself and your world. You will also develop a greater sensitivity and attunement with a sense of inner guidance and wisdom, which can serve you well in all aspects of your personal and professional development.

Following are a few starter questions to aid you on your journey of discovery. Pick a few of these reflective questions to play with. We suggest that you try doing this every day for a week. Many people find they gain insight and guidance through reflection at night or through keeping a journal or a diary. Such reflection can be a practical way of tapping into a source of inner wisdom.

If, after a week, you find that this process of daily reflection is valuable for you, you may want to do it on a regular basis. Such a decision will raise this practice quickly to the level of a habit. Making reflection a habit is a powerful way of allowing the process to gather strength and to work as a positive, empowering, and creative force in your life.

Reflections Concerning Events

1. What happened today that was meaningful or significant for you? Tell the story about it. What occurred? What stood out? What was important or significant about this for you?

2. Were there any humorous incidents today that illustrate a key learning that you want to remember?

This second question helps you see the humor and wisdom in your daily life. Just as taking a photograph enhances your appreciation and vision of life as you're living it, collecting stories also gives you something interesting and helpful to share with others.

3. Did anything occur today that changed your image of yourself or your view of the world? If so, what was it that violated your expectations or opened you up to a new way of seeing things? Did you see any new connections, possibilities, or opportunities for yourself? What helped you to see beyond limitations you had previously placed upon yourself?

Reflections to Increase Personal Awareness

1. When during the day did you feel most alive and energized? What was going on? Why do you believe you were you energized?

2. What did you enjoy doing during this day?

3. When during the day did it seem like time flew by for you? What were you doing?

4. What would you have liked to have had more of or less of in your life today? What would you like to have more of or less of in your future?

5. What did you notice yourself caring about or being moved by today? What does this tell you about what's meaningful and important to you?

6. What stories or implications did you find yourself remembering or reflecting on today about why you are a certain way or why the world is a certain way? What do these stories say about you? If they weren't true, how would this change things for you?

7. What stories have people told you, or have you seen on TV or in a movie or heard in a lecture or a workshop, that you

tend to recall on a frequent or regular basis? What significance do these have for you? Are these stories empowering in that they make you feel stronger and more capable, or do they have the opposite effect and make you feel constricted and fearful? Be aware of these stories and the impact they are having upon you in shaping and reinforcing your beliefs.

8.   If these were stories about someone else, what would it say about the main character?

Listening to the Stories Shared in Your Organization

1.   What stories do you hear in your organization? What stories did you hear about your company or co-workers today? What are their implications? What effect do you think these stories might have on others?

2.   What stories did you tell or repeat to others today? What message did they convey? Do these stories contribute to creating the kind of place you want to work in? Is sharing stories of this type in line with your intention and higher vision of the effect you want to have in your organization and in the world?

The stories we tell ourselves have profound effects. By choosing to believe them we give them the power of our belief. Stories we believe affect the way we feel, behave, and operate. Stories occur within a framework. In other words, they provide us with a perspective or a view of the world. On one hand, stories help us make sense of the world, yet they can also limit our vision and lead us down blind alleys. At times stories produce unwanted feelings or unfortunate results in our lives if we are not consciously aware of their meanings and implications. Be aware of the stories you are internalizing. Pay more attention to the good, inspiring, or empowering stories and less attention to the disempowering ones, based on how they affect you.

PERSONAL REFLECTIONS 2: USING STORIES AND STORYTELLING TO ENHANCE EFFECTIVE LEADERSHIP

In this section we offer suggestions on how leaders can harness the power of stories in leading others, building high-performance teams, and creating effective organizational cultures.

1. Stories are a powerful mechanism for conveying the values and beliefs that help create the organizational culture you desire. To this end, be aware of the stories and messages you are communicating and be careful to tell the stories that are supportive of the culture you want to nurture. What we pay attention to grows.

   Stories focus attention and highlight what is important and why, so take stories and storytelling seriously. Use stories consciously to communicate a vision, provide direction, display humanness, and strengthen the culture of your organization. Think specifically about what message you want to send to your organization.

   Are you clear about what you value and want others to value in your company? Select stories that exemplify and accentuate these values. For example, if you desire exceptional customer service, collect stories of your employees who provided great customer service and tell these stories whenever you have the chance. You can do this either informally in your talks and in meetings or more formally in company publications.

2. You can also create a powerful cascading effect in using stories by asking other leaders to share your stories and to have them share their stories with you. Soon you will have a repertoire of stories to convey at appropriate times. By doing this you will also help your managers to become more aware of their own stories and the messages they are already conveying. This cascading approach to storytelling

can galvanize a community, reinforce desired behaviors, and increase the efficacy of communication in your organization.

3. Let your life be a demonstration of your values in action so that the stories about what you say and do become the stories that illustrate the kind of company and culture you want to create. Be sure that whatever you say, you act accordingly. As a leader, people look to you and your life, and they will tell stories about what you say and what you do. Their observations will become the stories of your organization. Be conscious of the importance and power you have in creating the stories that reinforce and demonstrate the kind of culture you are trying to create. Walking your talk can and will help to create the culture you desire. Be sure that your stories are congruent with the kind of culture you are you are trying to build.

4. Stories are the invisible glue that holds an organization together or that can create doubt and uncertainty. By our very nature as communicative human beings, our conversations are filled with stories. Stories have impact whether or not we are consciously aware of the impact. We can choose to become more conscious of the implications of the stories we are hearing and telling ourselves both individually and within our organizations. Strive to become more aware of the stories told in your organization? Are they in line with what you want? What is the gap between the stories and reality, or the gap between what people say and what they do? What stories say is important. They often provide insight into the kinds of behaviors and values that are rewarded in an organization. Pay attention to them; they make a difference. What stories do you tell as a leader? What is the central message they convey?

5. Find out what is important to others from listening to their stories. You will gain greater insight into their motivations, strengths, and desires. This will also help you to

gain an appreciation of who they are as individuals. Leadership is a personal relationship with others. Stories help bring people and teams closer together.

6. As a leader you can create shared experiences and thus develop a set of shared stories. Off-site team-building sessions and adventures can be very valuable in this regard. Such events, and the stories that come from them, can become touchstones that you refer to and that reinforce understanding, alignment, and trust. You can then use these touchstones to draw strength from when difficult challenges face you and your team on the job.

   Some companies are beginning to include spouses in off-site meetings. This helps to create a feeling of inclusion and support for the family as a unit as well as for the team members. The support of spouses is an important element in the total picture of achievement with balance.

7. Stories can also be used to remind you of what you want to remember to be an effective leader. These reminders will vary from person to person, but the effect will be similar. For instance, a reminder story might be one that helps you remember to listen well. Stories can help us remember to celebrate others' strengths and accomplishments, provide a clear sense of direction, or help us remember to explain to the troops why we are pursuing a given course of action. You can use key stories as reminders to yourself of what is important to focus on in your role as a leader.

8. Another way you can work with stories is to make a list of "keeper" insights. Such a list makes the wisdom gained from your experiences memorable and easy to refer to. These "keeper" points will also help you remember stories when you need them.

About the Editors

⚔ **Marshall Goldsmith**, ranked by the *Wall Street Journal* as one of the top ten consultants in executive development, is editor or coeditor of many best-selling business books, including *The Leader of the Future* and *The Organization of the Future*. He was recently named Executive Director of the *Financial Times* Knowledge-Leadership Dialogue.

⚔ **Beverly Kaye** is president of Career Systems International and cofounder of the Influence Alliance, specializing in influence and negotiation. She is the author of several top-selling career management books, including *Up Is Not the Only Way* and *Love 'Em or Lose 'Em*.

⚔ **Ken Shelton** is chairman and editor-in-chief of Executive Excellence Publishing and publisher of *Executive Excellence* and *Personal Excellence* magazines. He is the author of *Beyond Counterfeit Leadership* and coauthor of *Real Success*.